Chartered Institute (
Management Accountant

C000162620

This book comes with free EN-gage online resources so that you can study anytime, anywhere. This free online resource is not sold separately and is included in the price of the book.

How to access your on-line resources

You can access additional online resources associated with this CIMA Official book via the EN-gage website at: **www.EN-gage.co.uk**.

Existing users

If you are an **existing EN-gage user**, simply log-in to your account, click on the 'add a book' link at the top of your homepage and enter the ISBN of this book and the unique pass key number contained above.

New users

If you are a new EN-gage user then you first need to register at: **www.EN-gage.co.uk**. Once registered, Kaplan Publishing will send you an email containing a link to activate your account - please check your junk mail if you do not receive this or contact us using the phone number or email address printed on the back cover of this book. Click on the link to activate your account. To unlock your additional resources, click on the 'add a book' link at the top of your home page. You will then need to enter the ISBN of this book (found on page ii) and the unique pass key number contained in the scratch panel below:

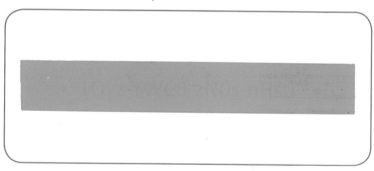

Then click 'finished' or 'add another book'.
Please allow 24 hours from the time you submit your book details for the content to appear in the My Learning and Testing area of your account.

Your code and information

This code can only be used once for the registration of one book online. This registration will expire when this edition of the book is no longer current - please see the back cover of this book for the expiry date.

Existing users

If you are an **existing EN-gage user**, simply log-in to your account, click on the 'add a book' link at the top of your homepage and enter the ISBN of this book and the unique pass key number contained above.

Professional Examinations

Paper C04

FUNDAMENTALS OF BUSINESS ECONOMICS

CIMA EXAM PRACTICE KIT

Published by: Kaplan Publishing UK

Unit 2 The Business Centre, Molly Millars Lane, Wokingham, Berkshire RG41 2QZ

Acknowledgements

We are grateful to the CIMA for permission to reproduce past examination questions. The answers to CIMA Exams have been prepared by Kaplan Publishing, except in the case of the CIMA November 2010 and subsequent CIMA Exam answers where the official CIMA answers have been reproduced.

British Library Cataloguing in Publication Data

A catalogue record for this book is available from the British Library

ISBN: 978-1-78415-289-5

Printed and bound in Great Britain.

CONTENTS

Quality and accuracy are of the utmost importance to us so if you spot an error in any of our products, please send an email to mykaplanreporting@kaplan.com with full details.

Our Quality Co-ordinator will work with our technical team to verify the error and take action to ensure it is corrected in future editions.

INDEX TO QUESTIONS AND ANSWERS

PRACTICE QUESTIONS

OBJECTIVE TEST QUESTIONS

SYLLABUS GUIDANCE, LEARNING OBJECTIVES AND VERBS

A THE CERTIFICATE IN BUSINESS ACCOUNTING

The Certificate introduces you to management accounting and gives you the basics of accounting and business. There are five subject areas, which are all tested by computer-based assessment (CBA). The five papers are:

- Fundamentals of Management Accounting

- Fundamentals of Financial Accounting

- Fundamentals of Business Mathematics

- Fundamentals of Business Economics

- Fundamentals of Ethics, Corporate Governance and Business Law

The Certificate is both a qualification in its own right and an entry route to the next stage in CIMA's examination structure.

The examination structure after the Certificate comprises:

- Operational Level

- Management Level

- Strategic Level

- Test of Professional Competence (an exam based on a case study).

B AIMS OF THE SYLLABUS

The aims of the syllabus are

- to provide for the Institute, together with the practical experience requirements, an adequate basis for assuring society that those admitted to membership are competent to act as management accountants for entities, whether in manufacturing, commercial or service organisations, in the public or private sectors of the economy;

- to enable the Institute to examine whether prospective members have an adequate knowledge, understanding and mastery of the stated body of knowledge and skills;

- to complement the Institute's practical experience and skills development requirements.

C STUDY WEIGHTINGS

A percentage weighting is shown against each topic in the syllabus. This is intended as a guide to the proportion of study time each topic requires.

All topics in the syllabus must be studied, since any single examination question may examine more than one topic, or carry a higher proportion of marks than the percentage study time suggested.

The weightings *do not* specify the number of marks that will be allocated to topics in the examination.

D LEARNING OUTCOMES

Each topic within the syllabus contains a list of learning outcomes, which should be read in conjunction with the knowledge content for the syllabus. A learning outcome has two main purposes:

1   to define the skill or ability that a well-prepared candidate should be able to exhibit in the examination

2   to demonstrate the approach likely to be taken by examiners in examination questions.

The learning outcomes are part of a hierarchy of learning objectives. The verbs used at the beginning of each learning outcome relate to a specific learning objective, e.g. Evaluate alternative approaches to budgeting.

The verb 'evaluate' indicates a high-level learning objective. As learning objectives are hierarchical, it is expected that at this level students will have knowledge of different budgeting systems and methodologies and be able to apply them.

A list of the learning objectives and the verbs that appear in the syllabus learning outcomes and examinations follows.

Learning objectives	Verbs used	Definition
1 Knowledge		
What you are expected to know	List	Make a list of
	State	Express, fully or clearly, the details of/facts of
	Define	Give the exact meaning of
2 Comprehension		
What you are expected to understand	Describe	Communicate the key features of
	Distinguish	Highlight the differences between
	Explain	Make clear or intelligible/State the meaning of
	Identify	Recognise, establish or select after consideration
	Illustrate	Use an example to describe or explain something

3   Application

How you are expected to apply your knowledge	Apply	To put to practical use
	Calculate/compute	To ascertain or reckon mathematically
	Demonstrate	To prove with certainty or to exhibit by practical means
	Prepare	To make or get ready for use
	Reconcile	To make or prove consistent/compatible
	Solve	Find an answer to
	Tabulate	Arrange in a table

4   Analysis

How you are expected to analyse the detail of what you have learned	Analyse	Examine in detail the structure of
	Categorise	Place into a defined class or division
	Compare and contrast	Show the similarities and/or differences between
	Construct	To build up or compile
	Discuss	To examine in detail by argument
	Interpret	To translate into intelligible or familiar terms
	Produce	To create or bring into existence

5   Evaluation

How you are expected to use your learning to evaluate, make decisions or recommendations	**Evaluation**	
	Advise	To counsel, inform or notify
	Evaluate	To appraise or assess the value of
	Recommend	To advise on a course of action

E COMPUTER-BASED ASSESSMENT

CIMA has introduced computer-based assessment (CBA) for all subjects at Certificate level. CIMA uses objective test questions in the computer-based assessment. The most common types are:

- multiple choice, where you have to choose the correct answer from a list of four possible answers. This could either be numbers or text.

- multiple choice with more choices and answers – for example, choosing two correct answers from a list of eight possible answers. This could either be numbers or text.

- single numeric entry, where you give your numeric answer e.g. profit is $10,000.

- multiple entry, where you give several numeric answers e.g. the charge for electricity is $2000 and the accrual is $200.

- true/false questions, where you state whether a statement is true or false e.g. external auditors report to the directors is FALSE.

- matching pairs of text e.g. the convention 'prudence' would be matched with the statement' inventories revalued at the lower of cost and net realisable value'.
- other types could be matching text with graphs and labelling graphs/diagrams.

In this Exam Practice Kit we have used these types of questions.

For further CBA practice, CIMA Publishing has produced CIMA eSuccess CD-ROMs for all certificate level subjects. These will be available from www.cimapublishing.com

F FUNDAMENTALS OF BUSINESS ECONOMICS

The assessment for Fundamentals of Business Economics is a two hour computer-based assessment comprising 75 compulsory questions, with one or more parts. Single part questions are generally worth 1–2 marks each, but two and three part questions may be worth 4 or 6 marks. There will be no choice and all questions should be attempted if time permits. CIMA are continuously developing the question styles within the CBA system and you are advised to try the on-line website demo at www.cimaglobal.com/cba, to both gain familiarity with assessment software and examine the latest style of questions being used.

G SYLLABUS OUTLINE

Syllabus overview

This paper primarily deals with the economic context of business and how competition, the behaviour of financial markets, and government economic policy can influence an organisation. It also provides the key microeconomic techniques underlying price determination and profit maximisation decisions.

The focus of this syllabus is on providing candidates with an understanding of the areas of economic activity relevant to an organisation's decisions.

Syllabus structure

The syllabus comprises the following topics and study weightings:

A	The macroeconomic context of organisations	25%
B	The goals and decisions of organisations	25%
C	The market system and the competitive process	25%
D	The financial system	25%

Assessment strategy

There will be a two hour computer based assessment, comprising 75 compulsory questions, each with one or more parts.

A variety of objective test question styles and types will be used within the assessment.

Learning outcomes and indicative syllabus content

C04 – A. THE MACROECONOMIC CONTEXT OF ORGANISATIONS. (25%)

Learning outcomes
On completion of their studies students should be able to:

Lead	Component	Level	Indicative syllabus content
1. explain the factors affecting the level of a country's national income and the impact of changing growth rates on organisations.	(a) explain determination of macroeconomic phenomena, including equilibrium national income, growth in national income, price inflation, unemployment, and trade deficits and surpluses;	2	• Changes to equilibrium level of national income using an aggregate demand and supply analysis. [5]
	(b) explain the stages of the trade cycle, its causes and consequences for the policy choices of government;	2	• Types and consequences of unemployment, inflation and balance of payments deficits. [5] • The circular flow of income, the main injections and withdrawals and their determinants. [5]
	(c) explain the consequences of the trade cycle for organisations;	2	• The trade cycle and the implications for unemployment, inflation and trade balance of each stage (recession, depression, recovery, boom). [5]
	(d) explain the main principles of public finance (i.e. deficit financing, forms of taxation) and macroeconomic policy;	2	• Government macroeconomic policy goals: low unemployment, inflation, external equilibrium and growth. [5] • Government policy for each stage of the trade cycle. [5]
	(e) describe the impacts on organisations of potential policy responses of government, to each stage of the trade cycle.	2	• Impacts of recession and boom on forecast sales of capital and consumption goods, industry profitability and employment levels in the firm. [5] • The main principles of public finance: the central government budget and forms of direct and indirect taxation, incidence of taxation (progressive, regressive) and potential impact of high taxation on incentives and avoidance. [5] • The main principles of public finance: fiscal, monetary and supply side policies, including relative merits of each. [5] • The effects on organisations of changes to interest rates, government expenditure and taxation. [5] • The effects on organisations of direct government macroeconomic policies including prices and incomes policies, labour market regulation, regulation on trade and policies to encourage investment. [5]

			Indicative syllabus content
2. explain the factors affecting the trade of a country with the rest of the World and its impact on business.	(a) explain the concept of the balance of payments and its implications for government policy;	2	• The main flows measured in the balance of payments accounts and the causes and effects of fundamental imbalances in the balance of payments. [6]
	(b) identify the main elements of national policy with respect to trade;	2	• Arguments for and against free trade and policies to encourage free trade (e.g. bi-lateral trade agreements, multi-lateral agreements, free trade areas, economic communities and economic unions), and protectionist instruments (tariffs, quotas, administrative controls, embargoes). [6]
	(c) explain the impacts of exchange rate policies on business.	2	• The effect of changing exchange rates on the profits of firms and international competitiveness of national industry. [6]
3. explain the influences on economic development of countries and its effect on business.	(a) explain the concept of globalisation and the consequences for businesses and national economies;	2	• The nature of globalisation and factors driving it (improved communications, political realignments, growth of global industries and institutions, cost differentials). [6] • The main trade agreements and trading blocks. [6] • The social and political impacts of globalisation (e.g. widening economic divisions between countries) and its influence on business (e.g. off-shoring), industrial relocation, emergence of growth markets, enhanced competition, cross-national business alliances and mergers). [6]
	(b) explain the role of major institutions promoting global trade and development.	2	• The impacts of modern information and communication technologies on international trade and patterns of development. [6] • The principal institutions encouraging international trade (e.g. WTO/GATT, EU, G8). [6]

C04 – B. THE GOALS AND DECISIONS OF ORGANISATIONS (25%)

Learning outcomes
On completion of their studies students should be able to:

Lead	Component	Level	Indicative syllabus content
1. distinguish between the economic goals of various stakeholders and organisations.	(a) distinguish between the goals of profit seeking organisations, not-for-profit organisations (NPOs) and governmental organisations;	2	• The forms of public, private and mutual ownership of organisations and their goals. [1] • Concept of returns to shareholder investment in the short run (ROCE and EPS) and long run (NPV of free cash flows) and the need for firms to provide rates of return to shareholders at least equal to the firm's cost of capital. [1]
	(b) explain shareholder wealth, the variables affecting shareholder wealth, and its application in management decision making;	2	• Impact on share price of changes to a company's forecast cash flows or its required rate using perpetual annuity valuations with constant annual free cash flows, or NPV calculations with variable cash flows over three years. [1]
	(c) identify stakeholders and their likely impact on the goals of organisations and the decisions of management;	2	• Role of stakeholders in setting goals and influencing decisions in organisations. [1] • Types of not-for-profit organisations. [1] • The status of economic considerations as constraints rather than primary objectives of not-for-profit organisations. [1]
	(d) distinguish between the potential objectives of management and those of shareholders, and the effects of this principal-agent problem on decisions concerning price, output and growth of the firm.	2	• The potential difference in objectives between management and shareholders. [1] • The principal-agent problem, its likely effect on decision making in profit seeking organisations. [1]
2. describe the behaviour of the costs of a product and service provider as volume changes and the implications for prices, competition and industry structure.	(a) distinguish between the likely behaviour of a firm's unit costs in the short run and long run;	2	• Changing efficiency in the short run (eventually diminishing marginal returns) and the long run (increasing and diminishing returns to scale). [2]
	(b) illustrate the potential effects of long run cost behaviour on prices, the size of the organisation and the number of competitors in the industry;	2	• Graphical treatment of short run cost and revenue behaviour as output increases using curvilinear and total cost curves. [2] • Long run cost behaviour and the long run average cost curve. [2]
	(c) illustrate the potential impact on prices and competition of e-business and globalisation.	2	• Increased competition and lower prices from the impact of e-business on costs of information search and by enabling low or zero variable cost. [2] • Impact on competition of the ability of business to source products and services from low cost emerging economies. [2]

Learning outcomes
On completion of their studies students should be able to:

Lead	Component	Level	Indicative syllabus content
3. calculate the level of output and price to maximise profits.	(a) demonstrate the point of profit maximisation graphically using total cost and total revenue curves;	3	• Short-run profit maximisation using graphical techniques. [2]
	(b) calculate the point of profit maximisation for a single product firm in the short run using data.	3	• Profit maximising output using data on price, quantity and unit costs. [2]

C04 – C. THE MARKET SYSTEM AND THE COMPETITIVE PROCESS (25%)

Learning outcomes
On completion of their studies students should be able to:

Lead	Component	Level	Indicative syllabus content
1. demonstrate the determination of prices by market forces and the impact of price changes on revenue from sales.	(a) identify the equilibrium price in a product or factor markets likely to result from specified changes in conditions of demand or supply;	2	• The price mechanism, determinants of supply and demand and their interaction to form and change equilibrium price. [4]
	(b) calculate the price elasticity of demand and the price elasticity of supply;	3	• The price elasticity of demand and supply. *Note:* calculate using arc and point methods. [4]
	(c) explain the determinants of the price elasticities of demand and supply;	2	• Influences on the price elasticities of demand and supply. [4]
	(d) identify the effects of price elasticity of demand on a firm's revenues following a change in prices.	2	• Consequences of different price elasticities of demand for total revenue, following price changes. [4]
2. explain the reasons for and effects of government intervention to stabilise prices.	(a) identify causes of instability of prices in markets for primary goods;	2	• Impact of periodic variations in output, short run inelasticity of supply, inelastic demand and the cobweb (or hog cycle) on price stability in primary markets. [4]
	(b) explain the impact of instability of prices on incomes of producers and the stability of the industry;	2	• Implications of price fluctuations for producer incomes, industry stability and supply. [4]
	(c) explain the effects on prices, producer revenues and market equilibrium, of government policies to influence prices in markets;	2	• Government price stabilisation policies; deficiency payments, set-aside, subsidies. [4] • Impact of employment costs. [4]
	(d) illustrate the impacts of price regulation in goods and factor markets	2	• Impact of minimum price (minimum wage) and maximum price policies in goods and factor markets. [4]

Lead	Component	Level	Indicative syllabus content
3. explain the main sources of market failures and the policies available to deal with them.	(a) explain market concentration and the factors giving rise to differing levels of concentration between markets, including acquisitions and combinations;	2	• Measures of market concentration and the impacts of market concentration on efficiency, innovation and competitive behaviour. [5] • Business integration including mergers, vertical integration and conglomerates. [5]
	(b) identify the impacts of the different forms of competition on prices, output and profitability;	2	• Effect of monopolies and collusive practices on prices and output, and profitability. [5]
	(c) explain the main policies to prevent abuses of monopoly power by firms;	2	• Competition policy and fair trading regulations. [5]
	(d) explain market failures and their effects on prices, efficiency of market operation and economic welfare;	2	• Positive and negative externalities in goods markets, merit good and demerit goods. [5] • Government response to market failure: indirect taxes, subsidies, polluter pays policies and regulation. [5]
	(e) explain the likely responses of government to market failures.	2	• Government response to market failure: Public assurance of access to public goods, healthcare, education and housing. [5] • Government response to market failure: Public versus private provision of services (nationalisation, privatisation, contracting out, public private partnerships). [5]

C04 – D. THE FINANCIAL SYSTEM (25%)

Learning outcomes
On completion of their studies students should be able to:

Lead	Component	Level	Indicative syllabus content
1. explain the causes of demand for finance and the assets used for borrowing.	(a) identify the factors leading to liquidity surpluses and deficits in the short, medium and long run in households, firms and governments;	2	• Finance for households: month to month cash flow management; short-term saving and borrowing; home buying; pension provision. [7] • Finance for firms: cash flow management; finance of working capital and short-term assets; long term permanent capital. [7]
	(b) explain the role of various financial assets, markets and institutions in assisting organisations to manage their liquidity position and to provide an economic return to holders of liquidity.	2	• Finance for government: cash flow management; finance of public projects; long term management of the national debt. [7] • Role of financial assets, markets and institutions: credit agreements, mortgages, bills of exchange, bonds, certificates of deposit, equities. [7]

Learning outcomes
On completion of their studies students should be able to:

Lead	Component	Level	Indicative syllabus content
2. explain the functions of the main financial markets and institutions in facilitating commerce and development.	(a) explain the financial and economic functions of financial intermediaries; [7]	2	• Role and functions of financial intermediaries: maturity transformation, risk management, aggregation, matching borrowers and lenders. [7]
	(b) explain the role of commercial banks in the process of credit creation and in determining the structure of interest rates; [7]	2	• Role and influence of commercial banks on the supply of liquidity to the financial system through their activities in credit creation. [7]
	(c) explain the role of the 'central bank' in ensuring liquidity and in prudential regulation; [7]	2	• Yield on financial instruments (i.e. bill rate, running yield on bonds, net dividend yield on equity), relation between rates, role of risk, the yield curve. [7]
	(d) explain the origins of the 2008 banking crisis and credit crunch; [7]	2	• Role and common functions of central banks: banker to government, banker to banks, lender of last resort, prudential regulation. [7]
	(e) explain the role of the foreign exchange market and the factors influencing it, in setting exchange rates; [7]	2	• Influence of central banks on yield rates through market activity and as providers of liquidity to the financial system as lenders of last resort, including by quantitative easing. [7]
	(f) explain the role of national and international governmental organisations in regulating and influencing the financial system; [8]	2	• The 2008 banking crisis and credit crunch: exposure to sub-prime debt, poor regulation, excessive lending. [7]
	(g) explain the role of supra-national financial institutions in stabilising economies and encouraging growth. [8]		• Role of foreign exchange markets in facilitating international trade and in determining the exchange rate. [8]
			• Influences on exchange rates: interest rates, inflation rates, trade balance, currency speculation. [8]
			• Governmental and international policies on exchange rates (exchange rate management, fixed and floating rate systems, single currency zones). [8]
			• Role of major institutions (e.g. World Bank Group, International Monetary Fund, European Central Bank) in fostering international development and economic stabilisation. [8]

EXAMINATION TECHNIQUES

COMPUTER-BASED EXAMINATIONS

TEN GOLDEN RULES

1   Make sure you are familiar with the software before you start exam. You cannot speak to the invigilator once you have started.

2   These exam practice kits give you plenty of exam style questions to practise.

3   Attempt all questions, there is no negative marking.

4   Double check your answer before you put in the final answer.

5   On multiple choice questions (MCQs), there is only one correct answer.

6   Not all questions will be MCQs – you may have to fill in missing words or figures.

7   Identify the easy questions first and get some points on the board to build up your confidence.

8   Try and allow 15 minutes at the end to check your answers and make any corrections.

9   If you don't know the answer, try a process of elimination.

10   Work out your answer on paper first if it is easier for you. Scrap paper will be provided for you. You are allowed to take pens, pencils and rulers with you to the examination, but you are not allowed pencil cases, phones, paper or notes, or a calculator.

Section 1

PRACTICE QUESTIONS

THE GOALS AND DECISIONS OF ORGANISATIONS

SCARCE RESOURCES

1

Fill in the blanks

(i) Economics is the study of the creation and distribution of ....

(ii) The fundamental problem in economics is the allocation of .... resources.

(iii) Where costs of using resources are minimised, this is known as .... efficiency.

(iv) Where resources are allocated to meet as many needs of the society as possible, we have .... efficiency.

(v) The benefit forgone by not using a resource in the next best alternative is known as .... cost.

(vi) An economy where all decisions are taken by the state is known as a .... economy.

(vii) An economy where all decisions are taken by individuals is known as the .... economy.

(viii) An economy which demonstrates some characteristics of a command economy and a free market economy is known as a .... economy.

(ix) Goods from the consumption of which the benefit derived for one consumer is not at the expense of the benefit for others are known as .... goods.

(x) There would be an underprovision if a .... good is left purely to market prices.

2

State three advantages of a centrally planned economy.

(i)

(ii)

(iii)

3

State three disadvantages of a centrally planned economy.

(i)

(ii)

(iii)

4

State four advantages of a free market economy.

(i)

(ii)

(iii)

(iv)

5

State four disadvantages of a free market economy.

(i)

(ii)

(iii)

(iv)

6

Factors of production	Reward
land	interest
labour	profit
capital	wages
enterprise	rent

Select the appropriate reward that goes with the appropriate factor of production.

(i)   interest and …………………

(ii)   profit and …………………

(iii)   wages and …………………

(iv)   rent and …………………

7

Economic growth brings about an increase in the output of an economy leading to an increase in living standards. Write down six conditions likely to promote economic growth.

(i)

(ii)

(iii)

(iv)

(v)

(vi)

8

In recent years, there has been a number of economists and others arguing against economic growth. State three valid arguments against economic growth.

(i)

(ii)

(iii)

THE BUSINESS ORGANISATION

9

State three constraints likely to be faced by an organisation.

10

What is a principal-agent problem?

11

Apart from profit maximisation, state three other possible company objectives.

12

Give four examples of not-for-profit organisations.

13

What are the 3Es?

SHAREHOLDER WEALTH

14

State four factors of production.

15

How are the following measures of financial performance calculated?

(i)   Return on capital employed

(ii)   Return on net assets

(iii)   Earnings per share

(iv)   Price/earnings ratio

16

The technique used to calculate costs and revenues in the future is known as?

17

What two elements of return might a shareholder expect from investing in a company?

18

State five factors which could affect the price of a share.

CORPORATE GOVERNANCE

19

Corporate governance is?

20

State three roles of shareholders in a company.

21

State four key responsibilities placed on the directors of the company.

22

How can shareholders lose control of a company they own?

23

State three advantages of share option schemes.

24

What was the Cadbury Report?

25

State five recommendations of the Cadbury Report.

26

What is the UK Corporate Governance Code?

27

Write down four features of a good corporate governance model.

COST BEHAVIOUR AND PRICING DECISIONS

28

Fill in the blanks

(i)   The .... run is the time period during which at least one factor of production remains fixed.

(ii)   In the .... run all factors of production are variable.

(iii)   .... costs do not vary in total as the level of output increases.

(iv)   .... costs vary in total in direct relation to changes in the level of output.

(v)   .... cost equals total cost divided by output.

(vi)   .... cost falls as production rises.

(vii)   Fixed cost + variable cost = ... cost.

(viii) Average fixed cost + average variable cost = ... cost.

29

Complete the following table from your knowledge of microeconomic theory and the information given below.

Quantity	Price	Total revenue	Fixed cost	Variable cost	Total cost	Average fixed cost	Average variable cost	Average total cost	Profit
0	–				200				
1	180				250				
2	170				300				
3	160				350				
4	150				400				
5	140				450				
6	130				500				
7	120				550				
8	110				600				
9	100				650				
10	90				700				

30

The following data refers to the costs of Firm A and the demand for its product.

Quantity	Price	Total cost
0	–	20
1	45	35
2	40	45
3	35	60
4	30	90

Using the table above, determine the output that maximises profit.

THE MARKET SYSTEM AND THE COMPETITIVE PROCESS

CONSUMER BEHAVIOUR AND DEMAND

31   PRICE ELASTICITY OF DEMAND

(i)   Price elasticity of demand (PED) is calculated by ....

(ii)   (a)   A perfectly inelastic demand curve would have a coefficient value of
                 ....

         (b)   A relatively inelastic demand curve would have a coefficient value between
                 .... and ....

         (c)   A unit elasticity demand curve would have a coefficient value of ....

         (d)   A relatively elastic demand curve would have a coefficient value between
                 .... and ....

         (e)   A perfectly elastic demand curve would have a coefficient value of ....

(iii)   The five factors which determine price elasticity of demand are

         1

         2

         3

         4

         5

32

Shifts in the demand curve are caused by

(i)

(ii)

(iii)

(iv)

(v)

SUPPLY AND THE MARKET

33 ELASTICITY OF SUPPLY

(i) Elasticity of supply may be calculated using the formula ....

(ii) Factors which affect elasticity of supply include

1

2

3

4

5

34

State three factors which would shift a supply curve to the left.

(i)

(ii)

(iii)

35

State three factors which would shift a supply curve to the right.

(i)

(ii)

(iii)

36

What is the difference between short run and long run in economics?

PRICE AND OUTPUT DETERMINATION

37 DEMAND AND SUPPLY

(i) If demand exceeds supply at a given price there is said to exist .... demand.

(ii) If supply exceeds demand at a given price there is said to exist .... supply.

(iii) If demand is equal to supply there is said to exist ....

38

(i) Give a reason why the imposition of a minimum wage might cause unemployment.

(ii) Give a reason why the imposition of a minimum wage might reduce unemployment.

39   MINIMUM PRICES

An agricultural market sells 1,000 sheep at a price of £50 per sheep. By means of a diagram explain the impact on price and quantity sold if the government set a minimum price of £65 per sheep.

40   MAXIMUM PRICES

The market clearing price for the rent of a two bed apartment is £500 per month. If the government imposes a maximum price of £400 per month, by means of a diagram show the impact on price and quantity of apartments now being rented.

LARGE SCALE PRODUCTION

41

Fill in the blanks

(i)   The level of output on the long run average total cost curve at which average costs first reach their minimum point is known as the ....

(ii)   A reduction in long-term average total cost is known as ....
....

(iii)   A rise in long-term average total cost is known as ....
....

(iv)   When a company introduces new products, this is known as ....

(v)   A .... is a combination of two companies on roughly equal terms with the consent of both parties.

(vi)   A .... is a combination of two companies, where one company acquires the other, sometimes against the wishes of the company which has been acquired.

(vii)   A merger between two motor manufacturing companies is an example of .... integration.

(viii) A merger between a textile manufacturer and a retail clothes shop is an example of .... integration.

(ix)   A merger between a construction company and a tobacco company is a ....
merger.

(x)   If a supermarket acquires a farm, this is an example of vertical integration
....

42

State five internal economies of scale which could arise if two large motor manufacturing companies merged.

(i)

(ii)

(iii)

(iv)

(v)

43

State three internal diseconomies of scale which could arise if two large motor manufacturing companies merged.

(i)

(ii)

(iii)

44

Production may be classified into three categories. They are

(i)

(ii)

(iii)

45

State three valid economic arguments in favour of a horizontal merger.

(i)

(ii)

(iii)

46

State three valid economic arguments in favour of a vertical merger (forwards or backwards).

(i)

(ii)

(iii)

47

Give two reasons why a merger between two companies in different industries would be beneficial to the new company.

(i)

(ii)

48

State two advantages and two disadvantages of specialisation.

Advantages

(i)

(ii)

Disadvantages

(i)

(ii)

49

Value for Money (VFM) is considered to be the best combination of services from the least amount of resources taking into account the 3Es. What or who are the 3Es?

(i)

(ii)

(iii)

50

State four reasons why conflict could exist between managers and shareholders in a company.

(i)

(ii)

(iii)

(iv)

MARKET STRUCTURE

51

Fill in the blanks

(i)   A person running their own business is known as a ………………

(ii)   Two or more people running a business without limited liability are running a ………………

(iii)   A business organisation regulated by The Companies Act and owned by shareholders with limited liability status is known as a ……………… ……………… ………………

(iv)   A company which is allowed to sell shares to the public has the following initials at the end of its name ………………

(v)   In a perfectly competitive market, all individual consumers and producers are said to be price ………………

(vi)   In a perfectly competitive market, products are said to be ………………

(vii)   The equilibrium of a firm operating under conditions of monopolistic competition where the average cost is still falling is operating at ……………… ……………… ………………

(viii) The main difference between monopolistic competition and oligopoly is that in oligopolistic markets there are ……………… ……………… ………………

(ix)   A monopolist has the ability to make ……………… profits in the long run.

(x)   The policy of pricing goods below their costs of production is known as ……………… pricing.

52

Although the model of perfect competition is hypothetical, it contains three economic optimal positions. What are they and what is the significance of them?

(i)

(ii)

(iii)

53

A monopoly exists when one producer controls the whole market. This is because there are barriers preventing other firms from entering the industry. State six types of barriers that can exist.

(i)

(ii)

(iii)

(iv)

(v)

(vi)

54

Price discrimination occurs where a product or service is sold at different prices in different markets. For price discrimination to work, the three conditions necessary are

(i)

(ii)

(iii)

55

Neoclassical theory suggests that all firms seek to maximise profits. In oligopolistic markets what other objectives might the firm have and why?

(i)

(ii)

(iii)

(iv)

56

What is a natural monopoly? Why might it be the case that a consumer might be better off in such a market?

57

Comparisons between perfect and imperfect markets.

	Perfect competition	*Monopolistic competition*	*Oligopoly*	*Monopoly*
No of firms				
Type of products				
Price competition				
Type of demand curve				
Information				
Barriers to entry				
Exists in real life				

Complete each column for perfect competition, monopolistic competition, oligopoly and monopoly.

THE PUBLIC SECTOR AND REGULATION

58

State six arguments in favour of nationalisation.

(i)

(ii)

(iii)

(iv)

(v)

(vi)

59

State five arguments in favour of privatisation.

(i)

(ii)

(iii)

(iv)

(v)

60

State six criticisms of privatisation.

(i)

(ii)

(iii)

(iv)

(v)

(vi)

61

What is the difference between a public good and a merit good?

62

Why do governments establish official bodies to regulate privatised utilities?

THE MACROECONOMIC CONTENT OF BUSINESS: THE DOMESTIC ECONOMY

NATIONAL INCOME

63

What are the three methods by which national income statistics can be calculated?

(i)

(ii)

(iii)

64

Why do countries bother to calculate national income statistics?

(i)

(ii)

(iii)

THE CIRCULAR FLOW OF INCOME

65

The Keynesian view of savings is that savings are what is left out of income after consumption. What other factors might affect the level of savings in an economy?

(i)

(ii)

(iii)

(iv)

(v)

66

State three assumptions or limitations of the accelerator model.

(i)

(ii)

(iii)

67

What are the three injections and three withdrawals in the circular flow of income?

Injections	*Withdrawals*
(i)	(i)
(ii)	(ii)
(iii)	(iii)

68

In a closed economy with no government sector, if current income Y is £100 million and the full employment level of Y is £125 million, how much would the government have to spend to reach the full employment level if the value of the marginal propensity to consume was equal to 0.8?

69

The paradox of thrift claims that an increase in the amount that households wish to save does not lead to an increase in the amount that is saved. How can this be possible?

70 THE TRADE CYCLE

The trade cycle shows the fluctuations in the level of economic activity over a period of time.

(i) When there is a slight downturn in the level of economic activity, this is known as ....

(ii) If the downturn continues for a longer period of time, it is known as ....

(iii) The bottom of the trade cycle is known as the ....

(iv) When the economy rises out of (iii) we have a period of ....

(v) When the economy grows at a fast level we are in a .... period.

71

State whether the following is true or false.

(i)   Higher interest rates will encourage spending.

(ii)   The marginal efficiency of capital is inversely related to the rate of interest.

(iii)   The accelerator states that an increase in consumer demand will reduce investment demand.

(iv)   Imports, taxes and savings are leakages from the circular flow of income.

(v)   Income equals expenditure at any point on the 45° line.

(vi)   The multiplier is where an injection into the flow of funds raises income by more than that amount.

(vii)   Demand management is advocated to counteract the trade cycle by Keynesian economists.

(viii) Household saving — disposable income — consumer expenditure.

INFLATION AND UNEMPLOYMENT

72

State two sources of cost push inflation and two sources of demand pull inflation.

(i)

(ii)

73

Inflation may be defined as the continuous increase in the level of prices resulting in a fall in the value of a given currency. Which groups gain and lose out to inflation?

Gainers	Losers
(i)	(i)
(ii)	(ii)
(iii)	(iii)

74

What is the quantity theory of money?

75

State five types of unemployment.

(i)

(ii)

(iii)

(iv)

(v)

76

State five causes of unemployment.

(i)

(ii)

(iii)

(iv)

(v)

77

What is the Phillips curve?

78

Give six examples of supply-side policies:

(i)

(ii)

(iii)

(iv)

(v)

(vi)

79

State four costs of unemployment.

(i)

(ii)

(iii)

(iv)

80

How do the Keynesians and monetarists disagree about the causes of unemployment?

MONETARY POLICY

81

The quantity theory of money states that MV = PT, that is, the supply of money = the demand for money, where

(i)   M is

(ii)   V is

(iii)   P is

(iv)   T is

82

What are the three main methods by which the Bank of England seek to control the money supply?

(i)

(ii)

(iii)

83

If the central bank were to increase interest rates, what would be the economic consequences?

(i)

(ii)

(iii)

(iv)

(v)

84

What was the theoretical basis for medium-term financial strategy?

85

What would be the value of the credit multiplier if the reserve asset ratio was

(i)   10%

(ii)   20%

(iii)   25%

(iv)   40%

(v)   50%

86

The figures below represent a simplified balance sheet of a clearing bank (A)

Assets		Liabilities	
Loans	£80m	Deposits	£100m
Cash	£20m		
	———		———
	£100m		£100m

The government decides to sell some government securities of which £5 million worth are purchased by customers of Bank A.

(i)   Reconstruct the balance sheet to show the impact of these purchases.

(ii)   Reconstruct the balance sheet to show that a reserve asset ratio of 20% has been maintained.

87

What is inflation targeting?

88

How might the effects of a change in the money supply differ between the short and the long run?

89

Explain the difference between the Keynesian and monetarist views of the following economic variables.

(i)   Demand for money

(ii)   Supply of money

(iii)   Interest rates

(iv)   Investment

(v)   Savings

(vi)   Government policy

90

What are the advantages of having an independent central bank?

(i)

(ii)

FISCAL POLICY

91

Adam Smith outlined four canons of taxation in the first economics book "The Wealth of Nations". They are

(i)

(ii)

(iii)

(iv)

92

Complete the following statements:

(i)   An indirect tax is levied on ....

(ii)   A direct tax is levied on .... or ....

(iii)   A tax levied as a percentage of expenditure is an ....
....

(iv)   The proportion of tax paid increases as income and wealth rise, this is an example of
a .... tax.

(v)   The proportion of tax paid decreases as income tax rises, this is an example of a
.... tax.

(vi)   Tax levied on company profits are called .... taxes.

(vii)   National insurance is an example of a .... tax.

(viii) Money received from a relative or benefactor upon their death is also subject to
taxation, this is known as .... tax.

(ix)   Tax levied on property in the United Kingdom is called .... tax.

(x)   Tax paid on certain items such as petrol, tobacco and alcohol is known as and
.... duty.

93

Over the past twenty years there has been a switch from direct to indirect taxation in the
United Kingdom.

Advantages

(i)

(ii)

(iii)

Disadvantages

(i)

(ii)

(iii)

94

State three reasons why a government might offer a certain type of producer subsidy.

(i)

(ii)

(iii)

95

The Public Sector Net Cash Requirement (PSNCR), has increased over the past few years. This is due to

(i)

(ii)

(iii)

(iv)

(v)

96

What is the Fiscal stance?

97

Why might monetarists worry about a government running a large positive PSNCR?

98

What is the difference between PSNCR and the national debt?

99

Why are economists more concerned with the relative size of PSNCR rather than the absolute amount?

GOVERNMENT ECONOMIC POLICY

100

What are the four macroeconomic objectives of government?

(i)

(ii)

(iii)

(iv)

101

What are the main instruments of economic policy?

(i)

(ii)

(iii)

(iv)

102

Give four examples of supply-side policies.

(i)

(ii)

(iii)

(iv)

103

State four methods by which government policy could increase economic growth.

(i)

(ii)

(iii)

(iv)

104

State three reasons why a government might offer a firm a subsidy.

(i)

(ii)

(iii)

105

Distinguish between marketable and non-marketable debt.

106

State four reasons why demand management might be ineffective.

(i)

(ii)

(iii)

(iv)

107

What factors can contribute to the downturn in an economic trade cycle?

(i)

(ii)

(iii)

(iv)

108

What is fiscal drag?

109

Which of the following statements are Keynesian or monetarist beliefs?

(i)   Supply creates demand.

(ii)   If the laws of supply and demand are allowed to operate, then wages will adjust to the full employment level.

(iii)   Fixed exchange rates make fiscal policy more effective.

(iv)   Market mechanism might work in the long run but in the long run we are all dead.

(v)   Inflation is the most important policy objective.

(vi)   Full employment is the most important policy objective.

(vii)   Monetary policy is more important than fiscal policy.

THE MACROECONOMIC CONTEXT OF BUSINESS: THE INTERNATIONAL ECONOMY

GLOBALISATION AND TRADE

110

State four advantages of free trade.

(i)

(ii)

(iii)

(iv)

111

Distinguish between absolute and comparative advantage.

112

If free trade leads to a higher standard of living, suggest four reasons why countries pursue protectionist policies.

(i)

(ii)

(iii)

(iv)

113

State four types of protectionism.

(i)

(ii)

(iii)

(iv)

114

What is a multinational corporation?

115

What are the arguments against protectionism?

(i)

(ii)

(iii)

116

What are the benefits of direct foreign investment?

(i)

(ii)

(iii)

(iv)

117

What are the practical limitations of international trade?

(i)

(ii)

(iii)

(iv)

BALANCE OF PAYMENTS

118

The balance of payments is a financial record of transactions between individuals, companies and government of one country with that of another. For the United Kingdom, it is customary to measure these figures over a calendar year. It is comprised of the following sections:

(i)   The .... account relates to tangible goods.

(ii)   The .... account relates to services, interest, profit and dividends.

(iii)   If we add together (i) and (ii) this gives us the .... account.

(iv)   Cross border changes in the holding of assets and liabilities is recorded in the .... account of the balance of payments.

(v)   If these totals do not add up properly there is an adjustment made which is called either the .... or ....

119

The following figures are available to you:

Exports	£10 million
Imports	£12 million
Invisible trade credit	£6 million
Debit	£5 million
Capital account balance	£500,000 inflow

(i)   Calculate the visible trade balance

(ii)   Calculate the invisible balance

(iii)   Calculate the balance on the combined current and capital account

120

Define the following terms.

(i)   Visible earnings

(ii)   Invisible trade

(iii)   Current account deficit

(iv)   Errors and omissions

121

What is hot money?

122

State three items which would appear as a surplus on the UK invisible balance.

(i)

(ii)

(iii)

123

Calculate the current account balance for the following 3 years.

	Visible balance	Invisible balance
	£m	£m
Year 1	−13,771	+2,972
Year 2	−13,378	+2,706
Year 3	−10,594	+8,411

(i)   Current account year 1 =

(ii)   Current account year 2 =

(iii)   Current account year 3 =

124

What is deindustrialisation?

125

What policy options can a government take if it is faced with a balance of payments deficit?

(i)

(ii)

(iii)

(iv)

126

Why are governments reluctant to use deflation to solve a balance of payments disequilibrium?

THE FINANCIAL SYSTEM

THE FINANCIAL SYSTEM

127

According to Keynes, there are three reasons why we hold money. They are

(i)

(ii)

(iii)

128

The factors which influence our demand for holding money are

(i)

(ii)

(iii)

129 BOND PRICES AND INTEREST RATES

The current market rate of interest is 10%. The government is issuing new bonds at £100 each offering a yield of 10%.

(i)   What would be the maximum price you would pay for the bond?

(ii)   If market rates of interest rose and the yield on the bond remained at 10% what would happen to the price of the bond?

(iii)   If market rates fall and the bond remained at 10% what would happen to the price of the bond?

(iv)   If interest rates were 5% what would be the maximum price you pay for the bond?

(v)   If interest rates were 20% what would be the maximum price you would pay?

(vi)   How much would the government redeem the bond for?

130

What factors would affect the rates of interest charged on a specific loan?

(i)

(ii)

(iii)

(iv)

(v)

131

The following financial data refer to an economy over a five-year period:

Interest rates	2000	2001	2002	2003	2004
Base rate	8.5	7.0	5.5	6.8	5.8
Instant access deposit rate	6.3	4.9	3.8	4.2	2.8
90-day access deposit	8.8	6.2	4.5	4.9	3.9
Mortgage rate	11.0	9.4	7.7	8.4	7.0

(i)   What is the base rate?

(ii)   What is instant access deposit rate?

(iii)   What is 90-day access deposit rate?

(iv)   What is mortgage rate?

(v)   Why is instant access rate below 90-day access rate?

(vi)   Why is mortgage rate higher than base rates?

(vii)   What is the difference between nominal and real rates of interest?

(viii) If the retail price index for 2000 shows a rate of inflation of 4%, what was the real rate of interest in that year?

132

There are three ways for the government to control the money supply:

(i)   Interest rates

(ii)   Open market operations

(iii)   Reserve asset ratios

If monetary policy were to be relaxed, which combination of policies would be appropriate?

A   Interest rates to be raised/cut

B   The government to buy/sell government securities

C   The reserve asset ratio to be reduced/increased

133   YIELD CURVE

The yield curve represents the term "structure of interest rates" which is concerned with the way the yield of a security varies according to the duration of the security. It normally slopes upwards. This can be explained in terms of

(i)

(ii)

(iii)

134

The following statements are either true or false

(i)   Precautionary demand for money is determined by interest rates.

(ii)   The price of a bond is inversely related to market rates of interest.

(iii)   According to the liquidity preference theory, the transactions demand for money is completely interest inelastic.

(iv)   Narrow money is more liquid than broad money.

(v)   The loanable funds theory is the monetarist view of how interest rates work.

(vi)   Banks will lend money to their good customers at base rates.

(vii)   A yield curve which rises from left to right indicates that interest rates are expected to rise in the future.

(viii) The nominal rate of interest is always above the real rate of interest.

(ix)   The higher the risks, the higher the rate of interest.

135

The major function of money is its function as a medium of exchange. What must money possess in order for this function to work.

136

The stock exchange has two roles. First, to raise new finance for companies and governments, and secondly, to provide a secondary market for investors. Who are the key institutional investors?

(i)

(ii)

(iii)

(iv)

(v)

137

The stock exchange runs four types of markets. They are

(i)

(ii)

(iii)

(iv)

138

What do the following initials stand for?

(i)   FTSE

(ii)   GEMM

(iii)   SEAQ

(iv)   TOPIC

(v)   CREST

(vi)   SEDOL

(vii) AIM

(viii) USM

(ix)   LIBID

(x)   LIBOR

139

Merchant banks, now referred to as Investment banks, offer the following services to customers:

(i)

(ii)

(iii)

(iv)

(v)

(vi)

140

In recent years the role of building societies is similar to that of banks, although three major differences still prevail. They are

(i)

(ii)

(iii)

141

State five characteristics of an investment trust.

(i)

(ii)

(iii)

(iv)

(v)

142

A unit trust performs a similar role to an investment trust but they are different. Three differences are:

(i)

(ii)

(iii)

143 VENTURE CAPITAL

The venture capital market exists to promote the growth of small businesses. This type of finance is equity rather than debt where the venture capitalists actually take a share in the business. The main providers of venture capital are

(i)

(ii)

(iii)

(iv)

(v)

144

There are several types of long-term capital. They include

(i)

(ii)

(iii)

(iv)

(v)

145

(i)   The most frequently quoted measure of the US stock market is the .... Index.

(ii)   The main share index in Japan is known as the .... Index.

(iii)   The money market used by the government when it requires short-term funds is the .... market.

(iv)   A market in sterling in which banks borrow and lend between themselves is known as the .... market.

(v)   A deposit with a bank in a currency other than that of the country in which the bank is located is called the .... market.

(vi)   Debt securities issued by listed companies is known as the .... market.

(vii)   The markets in (iv), (v) and (vi) are all examples of .... markets.

(viii) An unconditional promise to pay a certain amount of money at a given time in the future is a ....

(ix)   A bill of exchange with no supplier guaranteed by a bank is called a ....

(x)   A bill of exchange that has been accepted by an eligible bank or clearing house is known as an ....

FOREIGN EXCHANGE

146

Supply and demand for sterling against dollar/sterling exchange rate

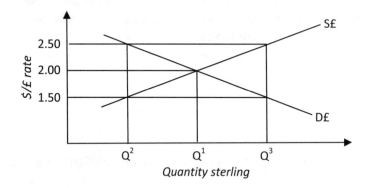

(i)   At an exchange rate of $2.50 = £1 is sterling over or under valued?

(ii)   If $2.50 = £1 was the fixed exchange rate would the Bank of England have to buy or sell sterling in the foreign exchange markets?

(iii)   What quantity would they have to buy/sell?

(iv)   What is the market rate of sterling against the dollar?

147

State three advantages of floating exchange rates.

(i)

(ii)

(iii)

148

State three disadvantages of floating exchange rates.

(i)

(ii)

(iii)

149

What is a managed or dirty float?

150

What is the purchasing power parity theory?

151

What are the economic forces and other factors which determine the demand for and supply of currencies?

(i)

(ii)

(iii)

(iv)

(v)

(vi)

152

In order to join the single currency, what was the convergence criteria member states had to fulfil?

(i)

(ii)

(iii)

(iv)

153

What is the overriding advantage and disadvantage of joining the single currency?

(i)   Advantage –

(ii)   Disadvantage –

154

State whether the following statements are true or false.

(i)   Free trade can benefit a country even if it has an absolute disadvantage in the production of the two commodities it produces.

(ii)   Governments determine exchange rates under floating exchange rates.

(iii)   The main argument in favour of a single currency is that it will reduce transaction costs within member countries.

(iv)   A country suffering from a deficit on capital account in the balance of payments and inflation should increase interest rates.

(v)   International trade leads to increased competition and higher prices.

(vi)   The imposition of a tariff on an imported car should lead to an increase in price and a reduction in the number bought.

(vii)   Imports are an injection in the circular flow of income.

(viii) A balance of payments surplus in the UK will lead to an increase in demand for sterling.

Section 2

OBJECTIVE TEST QUESTIONS

THE GOALS AND DECISIONS OF ORGANISATIONS

SCARCE RESOURCES

1   In a market economy, the allocation of resources between different productive activities is determined mainly by:

   A   the decisions of the government

   B   the wealth of entrepreneurs

   C   the pattern of consumer expenditure

   D   the supply of factors of production

2   The economy of the UK is best described as a

   A   command economy

   B   free market economy

   C   mixed economy

   D   socialist economy

3   In a market economy, the price system provides all of the following except

   A   a means of allocating scarce resources

   B   a signal to consumers

   C   a signal to producers

   D   an equal distribution of income and wealth

4   Which one of the following is not a social cost?

   A   passive smoking

   B   pollution

   C   traffic congestion

   D   the National Health Service

5   Which of the following is most likely to lead to a fall in a country's productive capacity?

A   an increase in technology

B   a fall in the population

C   the abolition of maximum hours laws

D   an increase in retirement age

6   Which one of the following is the best measure of the standard of living in a country?

A   the amount of savings in the banking system

B   the average weekly wage

C   gross national product per head

D   none of the above

THE BUSINESS ORGANISATION

7   All organisations exist to make profit.

True/False

8   Which of the following organisations is normally found in the public sector?

A   Education

B   Charities

C   Clubs

D   Businesses

9   The public sector is normally concerned with:

A   making profit from the sale of goods

B   providing services to specific groups funded from charitable donations

C   the provision of basic government services

D   raising funds by subscriptions from members to provide common services

10   In many companies, shareholders delegate control to the company's directors. In this context, a director is called an agent and a shareholder is called a _____.

11   A company which operates a policy of satisficing is

A   Attempting to maximise profits

B   Attempting to maximise sales revenue

C   Attempting to maximise market share

D   Attempting to seek acceptable levels of attainment for various stakeholder groups

12   Which of the following would be an example of a merit good?

(i)   Health

(ii)   Education

(iii)   Road Congestion

A   (i)

B   (ii)

C   (iii)

D   (i) and (ii)

13   Which of the following statements is correct?

A   Not-for-profit organisations are only found in the public sector

B   Not-for-profit organisations are only found in the private sector

C   Not-for-profit organisations can be found in both the public and the private sector

D   Not-for-profit organisations cannot survive without profits

SHAREHOLDER WEALTH

14   Over the past year the share price of X plc has increased from 120p to 150p. A dividend of 12p has also been paid. During the year the investor earned a rate of return of

A   15%

B   20%

C   30%

D   35%

The next two questions are based on the following information.

Dividend per share – 8.6p

Net profit after taxation – £17,000

Interest paid – £2,000

Number of ordinary shares – 70,000

Market price of share – 204p

15   The dividend yield is

A   8.6%

B   6.4%

C   4.2%

D   2.1%

16   The earnings per share is

A   15p

B   18.5p

C   19.7p

D   21.4p

17   An individual is expecting an income stream of £10,000 over the next four years. If a discount rate of 10% is to be applied, the level of income in Year 4 should be worth

A   £9,090

B   £8,260

C   £7,510

D   £6,830

18   If the central bank raised interest rates, the most likely outcome on the stock market would be?

A   A rise in share prices

B   A fall in share prices

C   No change in share prices

D   Impossible to tell

19   A credit card company charges me 3.5% interest per month. If I had a balance at the beginning of the year of £100 and did not make any payments during the year, how much interest would the credit card company charge me?

A   £150

B   £100

C   £51.11

D   £42

20   In the short run, companies will attempt to improve shareholder wealth by maximising:

A   Return On Capital Employed

B   Net Present Value

C   Normal profits

D   Average revenue

21   Earnings per share is measured as:

$$\frac{\text{Profit before interest and tax}}{\text{Number of shares}}$$

True/False

22 The main technique used to measure increase in shareholder value in the long run is:

A   Earnings Per Share

B   Return On Capital Employed

C   Discounted cash flows

D   Net profit

23 Earnings Per Share is sometimes used to make decisions about shareholder investment in the short run. What is the main weakness of this measure?

A   It is difficult to calculate

B   It varies depending on the profit achieved by the company

C   It does not measure change in shareholder wealth

D   It can only be calculated once each year

24 A project has the following cash flows:

Timing	0	1	2	3
Cash flow (£000)	(200)	750	500	(300)

Calculate NPV using a discount rate of 10% to the nearest £000.

A   1,095

B   670

C   1,520

D   425

25 An annual rent of £2,000 is to be received for ten successive years with the first payment due tomorrow. The relevant rate of interest is 8%. Calculate the present value of this stream of cash flows.

A   £15,420

B   £13,420

C   £12,500

D   £14,494

26 Define a perpetuity.

A   An annuity with an expected life of more than 20 years

B   An annuity that continues forever

C   An annuity with a discount rate of more than 10%

D   An annuity that starts in more than 20 years

27 **What is the main reason that NPV techniques are used to determine the impact of shareholder wealth of different projects?**

A   The increase in profit attributable to the shareholders is clearly shown

B   Shareholders are interested in cash, not profit

C   The directors can decide how much additional salary to pay themselves

D   The technique is easy to use at the time value of money is ignored

28 **The value of £1,000 to be received in one year's time at a discount rate of 10% is:**

A   £1,100

B   £1,000

C   £909

D   £890

CORPORATE GOVERNANCE

29 **The directors of a company are appointed by**

A   The shareholders

B   Fellow directors

C   Non-executive directors

D   Auditors

30 **The non-executive director is appointed by**

A   The executive directors

B   The non-executive directors

C   Shareholders

D   The chief executive

31 **Which of the following is not an advantage of share options?**

A   Managers are paid on a performance basis

B   Managers are more likely to take a longer-term view of strategy

C   Goal congruence with the shareholders

D   Directors will be able to practice insider dealing

32 **Which of the following is unlikely to be a cause of conflict between directors and shareholders?**

A   'Fat cat' salaries

B   Maximisation of short-term profitability

C   Maximisation of long-term cash flows

D   Mergers and acquisitions

33 **Which of the following is not normally seen to be an objective of corporate governance?**

A   Improving employee welfare

B   Increasing disclosure to stakeholders

C   Ensuring that the company is run in a legal and ethical manner

D   Increasing the level of confidence in the company for investors and shareholders

34 **Which of the following is not a principle of corporate governance according to the OCED?**

A   Disclosure and transparency

B   The rights of stakeholders

C   The role of directors

D   The equitable treatment of stakeholders

35 **One of the main benefits of corporate governance is improved access to capital markets.**

True/False

36 **Under the principles of good corporate governance, the CEO and chairman of the board will normally be the same person.**

True/False

COST BEHAVIOUR AND PRICING DECISIONS

37 **The table below shows the relevant costs of a firm at various outputs.**

Production	Total cost
0	£100
1	£120
2	£140
3	£160
4	£180
5	£200

The average fixed cost of producing 5 units is

A   £20

B   £100

C   £120

D   £200

38 **Diminishing returns occur in the short run because**

A   one factor of production is fixed

B   all factors are variable in the long run

C   of diminishing marginal utility

D   profits remain constant as output rises

39 **Diseconomies of scale occur when**

A   long run average costs begin to rise

B   long run average costs begin to fall

C   short run average costs begin to rise

D   short run average costs begin to fall

40 **Which of the following always rise when a manufacturing business raises output?**

(i)   total costs

(ii)   total variable costs

(iii)   fixed costs

(iv)   average costs

A   (i)

B   (i) and (ii)

C   (i), (iii) and (iv)

D   (i), (ii), (iii) and (iv)

41 **A business which satisfices will**

A   try to maximise profits

B   try to maximise sales

C   try to minimise unit cost

D   try to achieve a target which is acceptable to all parties

42 **Which of the following is not a function of profit in a market economy?**

A   a signal to producers

B   a signal to consumers

C   a return on capital

D   a reward for taking risks

43 **If a firm is enjoying economies of scale, then**

A   it is suffering from excess capacity

B   it must be a monopoly

C   it is maximising profits

D   unit cost is falling as output rises

44   A company doubles all of the input factors of production (land, labour and capital) and its output more than doubles. This is an example of:

A   decreasing returns to scale

B   constant returns to scale

C   increasing returns to scale

D   diminishing returns

45   The diagram below shows a Long Run Average Total Cost (LRATC) curve. The reason that the curve falls over output area A is due to the company experiencing economies of scale.

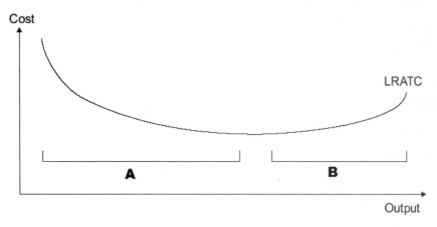

True/False

46   In the diagram below, the LRATC curve starts to increase over output levels B due to _____ of scale.

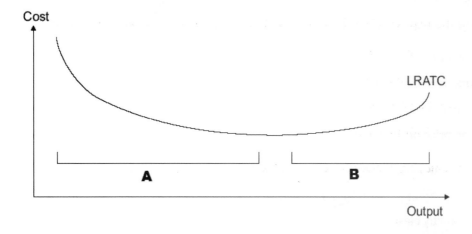

47   The long run average cost curve starts to rise after a certain level of output owing to:

A   economies of scale

B   diseconomies of scale

C   diminishing marginal returns

D   diminishing marginal utility

48 An example of an internal economy of scale that reduces the average cost per unit of production is:

    A   provision of backup services and industries

    B   specialisation of the workforce

    C   good transport links to customers and suppliers

    D   having a pool of specialised labour available to the company to hire

THE MARKET SYSTEM AND THE COMPETITIVE PROCESS

CONSUMER BEHAVIOUR AND DEMAND

49 From the demand schedule below, the price elasticity of demand following a fall in price from 25 to 20p is

Price	Quantity
30	15
25	20
20	25
15	30

    A   −1

    B   −1.25

    C   −1.50

    D   −1.75

50 Which of the following is not held constant when we draw the demand curve?

    A   the price of complementary goods

    B   the price of substitutes

    C   consumers' income

    D   the price of the good

51 If the price of a good fell by 20% but total expenditure on the good remained the same, the demand curve could be described as

    A   perfectly elastic

    B   elastic

    C   perfectly inelastic

    D   unitary elasticity

52   A demand curve is drawn assuming all but one of the following remains unchanged. Which item can vary?

   A   Consumer tastes

   B   The price of the product

   C   The price of other products

   D   Disposable income

53   Movement from P_0 to P_1 shows what?

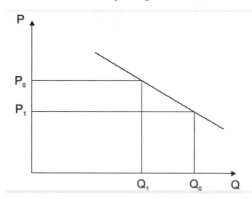

   A   An increase in the supply of the good

   B   A fall in the supply of the good

   C   An extension of demand

   D   A fall in demand

54   A normal demand curve is downward sloping because:

   A   customers derive more utility from the purchase of more units of a good

   B   customers derive less utility from the purchase of more units of a good

   C   companies require a lower profit margin as more of an item is produced

   D   companies require a higher profit margin as more of an item is produced

55   Complementary goods exist where:

   A   the purchase of one good means that a similar good is not purchased

   B   a number of goods exist, any of which can be purchased to satisfy a need

   C   one good is free and the other has to be paid for

   D   the purchase of one good leads to the purchase of another good

56   The demand curve for a good will shift to the right when:

   A   the price of the good falls

   B   disposable income increases

   C   the supply of the good increases

   D   the price of a substitute falls

57   The shift to the right in the supply curve on the diagram below can best be explained by:

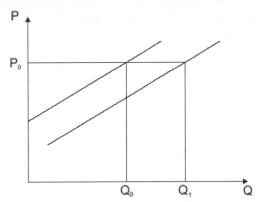

A   an increase in the price of the product

B   an increase in the price of raw materials

C   a rise in the amount of wages paid to labour

D   the result of technological progress

SUPPLY AND THE MARKET

58   A profit-maximising oil producer discovers that the government is to raise an extra 10% levy on his profits. In order to maintain profit maximisation, which policy would you recommend to him?

A   leave price and output the same

B   raise price by 10% and raise output by 10%

C   lower price by 10% and raise output by 10%

D   lower price by 10% and lower output by 10%

59   In the short run, a firm can continue to operate provided they can cover

A   fixed costs

B   total costs

C   average costs

D   variable costs

60   Which of the following would not shift the supply curve to the right?

A   a government subsidy

B   a government expenditure tax

C   an increase in technology

D   lower input prices

61   A farmer produces 1,000 tonnes of wheat with the government guaranteeing £50 per tonne produced. If the subsidy is increased by £5 per tonne and production rises to 1,200 tonnes, the elasticity of supply of wheat is equal to

    A   −1

    B   +1

    C   −2

    D   +2

PRICE AND OUTPUT DETERMINATION

62   The supply of agricultural products in the short run is

    A   completely elastic

    B   elastic

    C   inelastic

    D   impossible to determine

63   If the government set a maximum price below the market equilibrium price this will lead to

    A   excess demand

    B   excess supply

    C   market equilibrium

    D   none of the above

64   In the Common Agricultural Policy in order to reduce the butter mountains, a system of what kind was introduced?

    A   tariffs

    B   export subsidies

    C   quotas

    D   taxes

65   **In the diagram below, what action will suppliers take at the price of Phigh?**

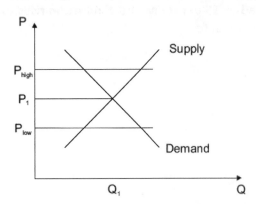

A   Increase supply to take advantage of the high price

B   Supply the same quantity of goods but at a reduced price

C   Supply a reduced quantity of goods but at the same price

D   Decrease price to attract more demand

66   **In the diagram below the equilibrium price for chocolate is P0 and Q0. What will the new equilibrium price be if people's incomes increase and chocolate is a normal good?**

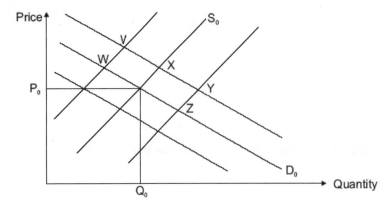

A   W

B   X

C   Y

D   Z

67   In the diagram below the equilibrium price for chocolate is P0 and Q0. What will the new equilibrium price be if there is technological progress in the chocolate-making industry?

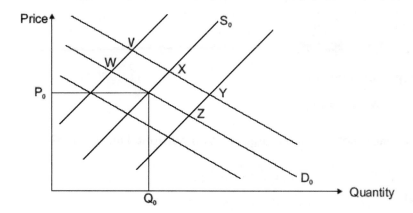

A   W

B   X

C   Y

D   Z

68   In the diagram below the equilibrium price for chocolate is P0 and Q0. What will the new equilibrium price be if there is an increase in the price of cocoa beans (an ingredient in chocolate)?

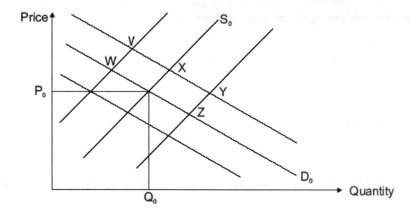

A   V

B   W

C   X

D   Z

LARGE SCALE PRODUCTION

69 **If Tesco plc acquired a food processing company, this would be an example of**

A   horizontal integration

B   vertical integration backwards

C   vertical integration forwards

D   conglomerate diversification

70 **Which of the following is not a strategic argument for horizontal integration?**

A   to increase market share

B   to pool technology

C   to achieve economies of scale

D   to reduce entry costs

71 **Which one of the following will tend to increase competition within an industry?**

A   barriers to entry

B   Government regulation

C   horizontal integration

D   low fixed costs

72 **Which of the following are examples of internal economies?**

(i)   technical economies

(ii)   financial economies

(iii)   trading economies

(iv)   managerial economies

A   (i)

B   (i) and (ii)

C   (ii), (iii) and (iv)

D   (i), (ii), (iii) and (iv)

73 **The Competition Commission was set up**

A   to create more jobs

B   to prevent regional inequality

C   to see how public interest was affected where one firm or more controlled the market

D   to improve industrial relations

MARKET STRUCTURE

74 **Which one of the following would act as a barrier to entry to a new firm trying to enter a market?**

A   perfect knowledge

B   consumer sovereignty

C   branding

D   low fixed costs of production

75 **Which of the following is an artificial barrier to entry?**

A   economies of scale

B   high fixed costs of production

C   Government issue of patents

D   price fixing

76 **Which of the following are examples of price discrimination?**

(i)   first and second-class rail fares

(ii)   business and economy class flights

(iii)   peak and off-peak rail fares

(iv)   a doctor charging wealthier clients higher consultancy fees

A   (i) and (ii)

B   (ii) and (iii)

C   (ii) and (iv)

D   (iii) and (iv)

77 **A natural monopoly may be beneficial to the consumer because**

A   the company controls a larger share of the market

B   the company can obtain economies of scale

C   the company can restrict output

D   none of the above

78 **All of the following are examples of anti-competitive behaviour by large firms except**

A   cartels

B   price fixing with retailers

C   offering retailers higher discounts if they do not stock competitors' products

D   extensive advertising

79 **Monopolies are always established by private firms.**

True/False

80 In the public sector, a monopoly will always obtain abnormal profits.

True/False

81 Monopolies tend to be inefficient regarding the amount produced because:

A supply always exceeds demand leading to waste of some goods produced

B production takes place where the MC curve is rising

C production cannot be increased without increasing price

D production is not at the lowest point on the ATC curve

82 In a monopoly situation, abnormal profits should attract more companies into the industry. What is the main reason this does not happen?

A Lack of information on the profits being made

B Insufficient consumer demand

C Barriers to entry into the market

D The Competition Commission restricts entry into the market

THE PUBLIC SECTOR AND REGULATION

83 A pure public good is one which

A no individual can be excluded from consuming it

B when consumed by one person implies less consumption by others

C involves no social costs in production

D is produced by the state

84 A chemical company has reduced the level of pollution from its factory. This will lead to a fall in

A social costs

B social benefits

C average costs

D marginal costs

85 Which of the following are examples of merit goods?

(i) defence

(ii) health

(iii) education

(iv) water

A (i) and (ii)

B (i) and (iii)

C (ii) and (iii)

D (ii) and (iv)

86 **A good which is characterised by both rivalry and excludability is known as**

A   a merit good

B   a public good

C   a private good

D   none of the above

87 **Which of the following is not an argument in favour of privatisation?**

A   a reduction in bureaucracy

B   a more even distribution of income and wealth

C   increased competition between firms in the same industry

D   greater consumer choice

88 **Which one of the following is not a valid economic reason for producing goods and services by the state?**

A   it is a merit good

B   it is a public good

C   it is a natural monopoly

D   it is a necessity which is consumed by everyone

89 **When privatisation took place in the United Kingdom**

A   assets were transferred from the public sector and money went to the government

B   assets were transferred from the private sector and money went to the government

C   assets were transferred from the private sector and money went to the private sector

D   assets were transferred from the public sector and money went to the private sector

90 **The production of a good results in a positive externality. The government should**

A   give the producer a subsidy which reflects the marginal benefit from the consumption of the good

B   give the producer a subsidy which reflects the marginal cost of the externality

C   impose a tax on the producer which reflects the marginal benefit derived from consumption

D   impose a tax on the producer which reflects the marginal cost of the externality

91 **The government may discourage horizontal mergers in manufacturing industry because**

A   by controlling the sources of supply, the merged firms will have unfair advantages over its rivals

B   the merged firms will be unable to secure economies of scale

C   consumers may lose out if the merged firm acquires market dominance

D   there is a lack of synergy between the two companies

92 **Cobweb theory attempts to explain:**

A   why prices in some markets are subject to periodic fluctuation

B   why companies in perfect competition must take the market price

C   why demand for some products fluctuates throughout the year

D   why there is a time lag between customers demanding a good and producers being able to supply that good

93 **There are many problems with market fluctuations, as explained in cobweb theory. Which of the following is not one of those problems?**

A   Frequent price shifts in essential commodities

B   Income uncertainty for suppliers

C   Imposition of appropriate taxation rates on the good

D   Inability to plan for major investment in the production of the good

94 **Which of the following is not a tool that the government can use to attempt to stabilise markets?**

A   Setting minimum prices

B   Providing guaranteed minimum income for producers in the market

C   Preventing over-production through set-aside payments

D   Setting a minimum wage

95 **A set-aside payment is the guaranteed minimum amount given to the supplier of a good to destroy the over-production of that good.**

True/False

96 **Which of the following goods is most likely to experience large fluctuations in supply due to the lag between change in prices and producers responding to that change?**

A   Motor vehicles

B   Air travel

C   Mobile telephones

D   Wheat

THE MACROECONOMIC CONTENT OF BUSINESS: THE DOMESTIC ECONOMY

NATIONAL INCOME

97 **Which of the following would underestimate the real value of goods and services?**

(i)   the existence of the hidden economy

(ii)   voluntary labour

(iii)   inflation

(iv)   capital consumption

A   (i) and (ii)

B   (ii) and (iii)

C   (iii) and (iv)

D   (ii) only

98 **Which one of the following is not a transfer payment?**

A   pension

B   student grant

C   family allowance

D   teacher's salary

99 **In which method of measuring national income statistics might you encounter double counting?**

A   expenditure and income

B   expenditure and output

C   output and income

D   output only

100 **An isolated community produces only one good, a newspaper, which sells 1,000 copies to a wholesaler at 50p per copy. The wholesaler then sells 500 copies at 70p per copy to each of the two newsagent retailers who sell the final copy to customers for £1 per copy. What is the community's weekly output?**

A   £500

B   £700

C   £1,000

D   impossible to determine

101 Why is GDP at market prices normally higher than GDP at factor cost?

  A GDP at factor cost includes exports and imports

  B GDP at factor cost excludes net property income from abroad

  C Taxes are normally higher than subsidies

  D GDP at factor cost is normally higher than GDP at market prices

THE CIRCULAR FLOW OF INCOME

102 The sum of the marginal propensity to consume and the marginal propensity to save must be equal to

  A less than 1

  B 1

  C more than 1

  D any amount between 0 and infinity depending upon the level of income

103 Which one of the following never constitutes an injection into the circular flow of income?

  A government expenditure on goods and services

  B the value of exports

  C investment by businesses

  D payment of VAT on goods and services

104 Consider the following information.

		£m
Exports	(X)	432
Investment	(I)	249
Savings	(S)	176
Government expenditure	(G)	329
Imports	(M)	503
Taxes	(T)	298

The national income of this economy will

  A start to fall

  B start to rise

  C remain static

  D be in equilibrium

105 **The acceleration principle states that**

A   the level of investment is determined by the rate of interest

B   the level of investment varies directly with the rate of change of output

C   an increase in output causes inflation

D   the marginal propensity to consume will rise with output

106 **National income is in equilibrium, where**

A   there is a balanced budget multiplier

B   planned injections — planned withdrawals

C   there is full employment

D   there is a balance of payments equilibrium

107 **The figures below show the consumption function for a given economy.**

Income	Consumption
£m	£m
100	95
120	110
140	125
160	140
180	155

The value of the MPC in this economy is

A   0.95

B   0.85

C   0.75

D   0.50

108 **A closed economy with no government sector has a marginal propensity to consume of 0.8 and a full employment level of £100 million. The current level of national income is £80 million. To achieve full employment, investment must rise by**

A   £4 million

B   £8 million

C   £16 million

D   £20 million

INFLATION AND UNEMPLOYMENT

109   Monetarists believe that inflation is caused by

    A   rising import prices

    B   trade unions demanding higher wages

    C   the government allowing the money supply to rise faster than productivity

    D   full employment

110   A deflationary gap exists where

    A   there has been a general fall in prices

    B   planned expenditure exceeds the full employment level of output

    C   planned expenditure is below the full employment level of output

    D   the time it takes for government deflationary policy to work

111   The original Phillips curve suggests that there is

    A   an inverse relationship between the rate of inflation and the level of unemployment

    B   a direct relationship between the rate of inflation and the level of unemployment

    C   an inverse relationship between the rate of inflation and the money supply

    D   a direct relationship between the rate of inflation and the money supply

112   Which of the following groups gain from inflation?

    (i)   Those on fixed incomes

    (ii)   Those who have index-linked incomes

    (iii)   Those who hold onto cash

    (iv)   Those who invest in non-financial assets

    A   (i) and (ii)

    B   (i) and (iii)

    C   (ii) and (iii)

    D   (ii) and (iv)

113   The money rate of interest in an economy is 5%. The rate of inflation is 7%. What is the real rate of interest?

    A   −2%

    B   2%

    C   5%

    D   7%

114 **A downturn in the level of economic activity is likely to lead to which type of unemployment?**

    A   seasonal

    B   frictional

    C   structural

    D   cyclical

115 **A reduction in the demand for coal and steel is likely to lead to which type of unemployment?**

    A   voluntary

    B   frictional

    C   structural

    D   cyclical

116 **An economy has a velocity of circulation of 10. It produces 10,000 goods with an average price level of £12.50. The money supply must be**

    A   10,000

    B   12,500

    C   15,000

    D   20,000

117 **The poverty trap exists in this country because**

    A   there is high unemployment

    B   at the lowest levels of income, marginal tax rates are in excess of 100%

    C   there is a North-South divide

    D   there is an ageing population

MONETARY POLICY

118

    (i)   a fall in the rate of inflation

    (ii)   a rise in the exchange rate

    (iii)   a rise in interest rate

    (iv)   an increase in the demand for money

    A   (i), (ii) and (iii) only

    B   (i), (ii) and (iv) only

    C   (i), (iii) and (iv) only

    D   (ii), (iii) and (iv) only

119   If the money supply is £25 million, and there are 500,000 spending transactions carried out on a weekly basis at an average price of £100 then the weekly velocity of circulation is

   A   1

   B   2

   C   3

   D   4

120   If the government were to pursue a contractionary monetary policy they would

   A   raise interest rates and sell securities

   B   lower interest rates and sell securities

   C   raise interest rates and buy securities

   D   lower interest rates and buy securities

121   The major impact of an increase in the reserve asset ratio would be

   A   to push up interest rates

   B   to reduce interest rates

   C   to reduce the level of liquidity in the banking sector

   D   to raise the level of liquidity in the banking sector

122   Which of the following is not a function of money?

   A   a store of value

   B   a medium of exchange

   C   a measure of value

   D   a hedge against inflation

123   If the Bank of England imposes a restriction on lending to property developers, this is an example of

   A   supply-side economics

   B   special directives

   C   open market operations

   D   Keynesian economics

124   A 3 year gilt has a redemption yield of 6% and a 20 year gilt has a redemption yield of 5%. This would suggest

   A   interest rates are expected to rise

   B   a normal yield exists

   C   an inverse yield exists

   D   long term interest rates are higher than short term rates

FISCAL POLICY

125   **Which one of the following can be used by government to finance a public sector borrowing requirement (PSBR)?**

A   an increase in interest rates

B   a rise in direct taxation

C   an increase in stamp duty

D   an issue of government savings certificates

126   **A progressive tax is one where the tax payment**

A   rises as income increases

B   falls as income increases

C   is a constant proportion of expenditure

D   rises at a faster rate than income increases

127   **The Public Sector Net Cash Requirement is best described as**

A   the accumulated debts of the government

B   the total amount borrowed by the banking sector

C   the amount required to finance a balance of payments deficit

D   the amount borrowed by the government and public authorities in a given period

128   **The burden of an indirect tax will fall more heavily on the consumer when**

A   the greater is the price elasticity of demand for the good

B   the lower is the price elasticity of demand for the good

C   the greater is the income elasticity of demand for the good

D   the lower is the price elasticity of supply

129   **If the government wishes to pursue an expansionary fiscal policy it should**

A   increase taxes, increase government expenditure

B   increase taxes, reduce government expenditure

C   reduce taxes, increase government expenditure

D   reduce taxes, reduce government expenditure

130   **Which of the following is not an expenditure tax?**

A   VAT

B   Excise Duties

C   Customs Duties

D   National Insurance

131 **Which of the following is not in Adam Smith's canons of taxation?**

A   convenience

B   equitable

C   objectivity

D   economy

132 **Which of the following is not a reason why a government should have a budget deficit?**

A   political commitments

B   an ageing population

C   a downturn in the level of economic activity

D   a fall in unemployment

133 **Which of the following would not follow an increase in government borrowing according to the monetarist view?**

A   higher interest rates

B   higher inflation

C   higher economic growth

D   lower investment

GOVERNMENT ECONOMIC POLICY

134 **Which of the following is never an objective of government economic policy?**

A   stable prices

B   fiscal policy

C   full employment

D   balance of payments equilibrium

135 **Which of the following is not an example of a supply-side policy?**

A   increased spending on training

B   privatisation

C   increased unemployment benefit

D   reduced direct taxation

136   Which of the following are examples of government marketable debt?

   (i)   Treasury bills

   (ii)   Gilt-edged stocks

   (iii)   National savings certificates

   (iv)   Premium bonds

   A   (i) and (ii)

   B   (i) and (iii)

   C   (ii) and (iv)

   D   (iii) and (iv)

137   Which one of the following measures would be expected to reduce the level of unemployment?

   A   an increase in value-added tax

   B   a balanced budget

   C   a reduction in employers' national insurance contributions

   D   a rise in the value of the exchange rate

138   A television licence is an example of a

   A   Regressive tax

   B   Progressive tax

   C   Direct tax

   D   None of the above

139   The total yield from an indirect tax levied on a good is likely to be highest when

   A   demand is inelastic, supply is elastic

   B   demand is inelastic, supply is inelastic

   C   demand is elastic, supply is elastic

   D   demand is elastic, supply is inelastic

140   Which of the following government policies would not raise the long-term rate of economic growth?

   A   encouraging a higher level of business investment

   B   increasing expenditure on education and training

   C   providing tax relief for companies engaged in research and development

   D   trying to encourage a greater amount of consumers' expenditure

141   Governments wish to control inflation because

    A   it redistributes from rich to poor people

    B   it damages international competitiveness

    C   it reduces government tax revenue

    D   it reduces unemployment

142   If governments were seeking to reduce unemployment, they should

    A   reduce interest rates, raise taxes

    B   reduce interest rates, lower taxes

    C   increase interest rates, lower taxes

    D   increase interest rates, raise taxes

143   Which of the following is not an argument in favour of a minimum wage?

    A   it seeks to eliminate the poverty trap

    B   it seeks to prevent voluntary unemployment

    C   it prevents people from working below the minimum wage

    D   it seeks a more favourable distribution of income and wealth

GLOBALISATION AND TRADE

144   The theory of comparative advantage states that

    A   A country will only benefit from trade in the production of a good in which it has an absolute advantage

    B   A country will export labour intensive goods and import capital intensive goods

    C   A country can benefit from trade even if they have an absolute disadvantage in all commodities

    D   Foreign trade should be viewed with suspicion

145   Which of the following is not an example of protectionism?

    A   Export subsidy

    B   Fixed exchange rate

    C   Import quota

    D   Import tariff

146   Why do countries impose tariffs on foreign goods?

    A   To prevent unemployment overseas

    B   To prevent unemployment at home

    C   To encourage free trade

    D   To help lesser developed countries

147 **A customs union is**

A   an area of the world where you pay no tax

B   an area with the same unit of currency

C   a free trade area which requires fixed exchange rates between member countries

D   a free trade area within a certain group of countries who have a common tariff with the rest of the world

148 **An increase in the international mobility of factors of production leads to**

A   an increase in international trade

B   increased unemployment in low wage economies

C   increasing differences in wage rates between countries

D   decreasing differences in factor prices between countries

149 **A multinational company is best described as one which**

A   sells its output in more than one country

B   produces goods and services in more than one country

C   is owned by shareholders in more than one country

D   has a product-based structure

150 **Which of the following statements is false?**

A   International trade allows countries to specialise

B   International trade allows consumers to a wider range of goods and services

C   International trade brings about economies of scale

D   International trade leads to international competition and higher prices

151 **In country A it takes 10 hours of labour to make one unit of x and 5 hours to make one unit of y.**

In country B it takes 6 hours of labour to make one unit of x and 9 hours to make one unit of y.

Which of the following statements is correct?

A   Country A has a comparative advantage in the production of both goods

B   Country B has an absolute advantage in the production of x and country A has a comparative advantage in the production of good x

C   Country B has an absolute advantage in the production of both goods

D   Country A has an absolute advantage in the production of both goods

BALANCE OF PAYMENTS

152 If the elasticity of demand for British exports is −2, then a devaluation of sterling should lead to

    A   a fall in the value of exports

    B   an increase in the value of imports

    C   an increase in the total foreign currency expenditure on British goods

    D   British goods becoming more expensive overseas

153 **Consider the following figures**

Tangible exports	£35,432 million
Tangible imports	£36,607 million
Invisible balance	£1,429 million
Current account	£354 million
Capital account	−£2,227 million

The visible trade balance was:

    A   −£1,175 million

    B   +£254 million

    C   −£1,126 million

    D   +£1,973 million

154 **Which of the following must always balance?**

    A   The balancing item

    B   The invisible balance

    C   The balance on current account

    D   The balance of payments

155 ICI based in the UK have a subsidiary in France. Last year this French subsidiary made £10 million profit of which £5 million was invested in France and the remainder came back to the UK. They decide to invest a further £15 million in France of which £10 million came from the parent company and £5 million was raised in France. The total currency flow for the UK was

    A   an outflow of £10 million

    B   an inflow of £10 million

    C   an outflow of £5 million

    D   an inflow of £5 million

156 Which one of the following will appear in the financial account of the balance of payments?

A   The export of whisky

B   The purchase of Euros to go on a Spanish holiday

C   Interest received on a United States government bond

D   Inflow of investment by Sony into the UK

157 A balance of payments deficit is least likely to be corrected by

A   imposing tariffs

B   increasing the value of sterling

C   reducing the level of aggregate demand

D   discouraging imports

THE FINANCIAL SYSTEM

THE FINANCIAL SYSTEM

158 Speculative demand for money is a function of

A   income

B   wealth

C   interest rates

D   the nature of the individual

159 If the central bank pursues an expansionary open market operations policy, it will

A   sell securities on the open market

B   buy securities from non-government holders

C   increase the reverse asset ratio

D   decrease the reserve asset ratio

160 If a bank buys a bill of exchange worth £100 in 3 months time for £96, the discount rate would be approximately

A   4%

B   16%

C   20%

D   24%

161   Which of the following is never an asset of a clearing bank?

A   cash

B   loans made to a company

C   a customer's deposit account

D   balances held with the Bank of England

162   In the Keynesian theory of demand for money, the transactions demand for money is determined by

A   the rate of interest

B   the level of consumers' income

C   expected changes in equity prices

D   the amount of money in circulation

163   The crowding out effect is caused by

A   a rise in interest rates reducing private sector investment

B   a rise in interest rates reducing public sector investment

C   a fall in interest rates reducing savings

D   a rise in interest rates raising mortgage rates

164   If the reserve asset ratio was 25%, how much money could a bank create from an initial deposit of £100?

A   £100

B   £200

C   £300

D   £400

165   If the market rate of interest falls, the price of bonds will

A   rise

B   fall

C   stay the same

D   could go up or down

166   Lenders normally want to lend funds for a short period of time but most borrowers want to borrow funds for a long period of time. Resolving this mis-match is known as:

A   pooling

B   aggregation

C   risk reduction

D   maturity transformation

167 **What is the main reason that borrowers and lenders are unlikely to contact each other directly?**

    A   Lack of communication systems

    B   High costs

    C   Financial intermediaries are only open for a limited amount of time each day

    D   They are unlikely to have assets that can be traded

168 **One of the roles carried out by financial intermediaries is to pool many small deposits to provide larger loans. The principle of pooling small deposits is called _____.**

169 **Which of the following is not a role of a financial intermediary?**

    A   Risk enhancement

    B   Aggregation

    C   Maturity transformation

    D   Financial intermediation

170 **Which of the following is likely to be a reason for short-term savings?**

    A   Holiday

    B   House

    C   Hair cut

    D   Pension

171 **In the short term, there is a lack of synchronisation between receipts and payments. Most people manage this problem by using a mortgage.**

    True/False

172 **A company faces seasonal demand for its products. Short-term borrowing will be required to help the company:**

    A   pay the annual dividend

    B   finance its existing loans

    C   purchase new machinery

    D   increase its stock levels

173 **Government organisations do not experience short-term timing differences between receipts and payments.**

    True/False

174   **Liquidity is defined as the ability to:**

A   convert assets into cash

B   save

C   convert paper money into gold

D   convert cash into goods and services

175   **Which of the following is not a characteristic of good money?**

A   It is durable

B   It is generally accepted

C   It is in unlimited supply

D   It is portable

176   **The main way of distinguishing between capital and money markets is by:**

A   transaction costs

B   the amounts involved

C   the time to maturity

D   the amount of risk

177   **Which of the following is unlikely to be traded on the capital markets?**

A   Equities

B   Bonds

C   Bills of exchange

D   Mortgages

178   **The ownership of companies is conveyed via _____ shares.**

179   **Which ONE of the following is a characteristic of ordinary shares?**

A   They provide the same rate of dividend each year

B   They can increase and decrease in value

C   They will be repurchased by the company after a given amount of time (normally 25 years)

D   They can be sold easily

180   **Bonds are normally issued at a premium although they are redeemed at par.**

True/False

181 **What does the nominal value of a bond signify?**

  A   The amount the bond was issued for

  B   The amount the bond is currently worth

  C   The amount it will be worth on redemption

  D   The amount of interest payable each year

182 **A certificate of deposit is an amount, above £50,000, that has been deposited with a bank for a fixed period of time and will be repaid with interest at the end of the term.**

  True/False

183 **An arrangement whereby one party borrows or takes possession of something in return for a future payment is called a _____ _____.**

184 **Which of the following is NOT a characteristic of a mortgage?**

  A   It provides a return of interest

  B   The lender expects security in the form of an asset

  C   It is a long-term agreement, lasting for up to 35 years

  D   It can be sold by the lender

185 **Which of the following is a characteristic of a bill of exchange?**

  A   No interest

  B   Very risky as there is no guarantor

  C   Medium-term instrument of between 1 and 5 years

  D   Cannot be resold

186 **Which of the following does not engage in the buying and selling of shares in other companies?**

  A   Unit trusts

  B   Investment trusts

  C   Pension funds

  D   The Stock Exchange

187 **Which of the following institutions does not invest in the capital markets?**

  A   Pension funds

  B   Unit trusts

  C   Insurance companies

  D   Discount houses

188   Equity finance in high-risk enterprises is known as

A   Venture capital

B   Working capital

C   Debentures

D   A bill of exchange

189   In the international capital markets, long-term capital would be supplied by the

A   Eurobond market

B   Eurocredit market

C   Eurocurrency market

D   The stock market

190   Which of the following is not a source of long-term capital?

A   Debentures

B   Preference shares

C   Factoring

D   Convertible stocks

FOREIGN EXCHANGE

191   The main advantage of a system of flexible or floating exchange rates is that it:

A   provides certainty for those engaged in international trade

B   provides automatic correction of balance of payments

C   reduces international transaction costs

D   provides discipline for government economic management

192   Which of the following is not a function of the World Trade Organisation (WTO)?

A   providing finance for countries with a balance of payments deficit

B   encouraging countries to reduce tariffs

C   encouraging free trade areas

D   discouraging non-tariff barriers

193   **A devaluation of the exchange rate for a country's currency will normally result in**

   (i)   a reduction in the current account deficit

   (ii)   an improvement in the country's terms of trade

   (iii)   a reduction in the domestic cost of living

   (iv)   an increased level of domestic economic activity

   A   (i) and (ii) only

   B   (i) and (iv) only

   C   (ii) and (iii) only

   D   (ii) and (iv) only

194   **Which of the following is not a benefit of a single currency?**

   A   reduced transaction costs

   B   lower interest rates

   C   reduced exchange rate uncertainty

   D   increased price transparency

195   **Which one of the following would likely lead to a fall in the value of sterling against the dollar?**

   A   a rise in UK interest rates

   B   a rise in US interest rates

   C   the Bank of England buying sterling for dollars

   D   capital investment flows from New York to London

196   **The current rate of exchange between the UK and the United States is £1 = $1.50. The sterling price of a Jaguar car is £100,000. If the exchange rate moves to £1 = $1.40 and the sterling price remains the same, what will be the new dollar price of the car?**

   A $100,000

   B $140,000

   C $150,000

   D $160,000

197   **The major disadvantage of a single currency to an individual country is:**

   A   loss of monetary control

   B   loss of fiscal control

   C   higher transaction costs

   D   none of the above

198 Which one of the following shows the lowest degree of international mobility within Europe?

A   management

B   capital

C   technology

D   unskilled labour

199 The advantage of fixed exchange rates include:

(i)   monetary policy is more effective

(ii)   fiscal policy is more effective

(iii) there will be no need to hold reserves

A   (i) and (ii)

B   (i) and (iii)

C   (ii) and (iii)

D   (ii) only

200 Which of the following is unlikely to affect the demand for sterling?

A   An increase in UK exports

B   An increase in UK imports

C   Government intervention to support the exchange rate

D   Overseas investors making investments in the UK

Section 3

ANSWERS TO PRACTICE QUESTIONS

THE GOALS AND DECISIONS OF ORGANISATIONS

SCARCE RESOURCES

1

- (i)   wealth
- (ii)   scarce
- (iii)   technical
- (iv)   allocative
- (v)   opportunity
- (vi)   command
- (vii)   free market
- (viii) mixed
- (ix)   public
- (x)   merit

2

- (i)   no unemployment
- (ii)   basic needs catered for
- (iii)   weaker members of society catered for

3

- (i)   lack of incentives
- (ii)   existence of black markets
- (iii)   organisations become too bureaucratic

4

    (i)   system responds to consumer preferences

    (ii)   people have freedom of choice

    (iii)   competition ensures technical efficiency

    (iv)   consumers ensure there is allocative efficiency

5

    (i)   unequal distribution of income and wealth

    (ii)   no supply of public and merit goods

    (iii)   unemployment

    (iv)   social costs

6

    (i)   capital

    (ii)   enterprise

    (iii)   labour

    (iv)   land

7

    (i)   technology

    (ii)   flexible and educated workforce

    (iii)   investment in infrastructure

    (iv)   availability of capital

    (v)   political stability

    (vi)   good working environment

8

    (i)   not sustainable if it is based on consumption of finite resources

    (ii)   causes pollution and environmental damage

    (iii)   global dominance by large multinationals

THE BUSINESS ORGANISATION

9

    (i)   The law

    (ii)   The nature of the business

    (iii)   Human nature

10

A principal-agent problem emerges when the shareholders, that is principals, contract another party, that is managers or agents, to carry out tasks on their behalf. Thus, the objectives of the business may be determined by the agents.

11

    (i)   Sales maximisation

    (ii)   Satisficing

    (iii)   Market share

12

    (i)   A charity

    (ii)   Local government

    (iii)   A social club

    (iv)   A regulatory body

13

    (i)   Economy

    (ii)   Efficiency

    (iii)   Effectiveness

SHAREHOLDER WEALTH

14

    (i)   Land

    (ii)   Labour

    (iii)   Capital

    (iv)   Entrepreneurship

15

    (i) $\text{ROCE} = \dfrac{\text{Profit before interest and tax}}{\text{Average capital employed}} \times 100$

    (ii) $\text{Return on net assets} = \dfrac{\text{Operating profit (before interest and tax)}}{\text{Total assets - current liabilitie s}} \times 100$

    (iii) $\text{EPS} = \dfrac{\text{Earnings per share}}{\text{Market price of share}} \times 100$

    (iv) $\text{P/E ratio} = \dfrac{\text{Current market price of share}}{\text{EPS at the last publicatio n of results}}$

16

Discounted cash flow technique

17

(i)   Dividend

(ii)   Rise in market share price

18

(i)   Profits

(ii)   Speculation

(iii)   Merger/takeover

(iv)   Recession

(v)   Interest rates

CORPORATE GOVERNANCE

19

The system by which companies and other organisations are directed and controlled.

20

(i)   Appoint the directors of the company

(ii)   Appoint the auditors for the company

(iii)   Assure themselves that the system of governance is appropriate and effective

21

(i)   To determine the broad long-term aims of the company

(ii)   To provide a focus of leadership

(iii)   To supervise the management of the company

(iv)   To report to shareholders on the performance of the company

22

(i)   Organisations become too large

(ii)   Organisations become too complex

(iii)   Individual shareholders have minority interest

23

(i)   Managers are paid on a performance-related basis

(ii)   Managers take a longer-term view of the organisation's strategy

(iii)   Goal congruence with other shareholders

24

It was based on a committee set up by the Stock Exchange because of the concern over corporate governance. The task of the committee chaired by Sir Adrian Cadbury was to review the process of corporate governance in the U.K.

25

(i)   Board of directors should meet on a regular basis

(ii)   Directors should have limited period contracts (3 year)

(iii)   Greater involvement of non-executive directors

(iv)   Directors reward to be publicly disclosed

(v)   Statement made in annual report stating whether company adheres to Cadbury Report recommendations

26

The UK Corporate Governance Code is basically a review of all corporate governance issues which have been raised since the Cadbury Committee. They believe the way forward is for companies to pursue a policy of 'best practice'.

27

(i)   Separation of power especially the role of chairman and chief executive

(ii)   An appropriate balance of executive and non-executive directors

(iii)   The adoption of the principles of transparency, openness and fairness

(iv)   To ensure that the board of directors are fully accountable

COST BEHAVIOUR AND PRICING DECISIONS

28

(i)   short

(ii)   long

(iii)   fixed

(iv)   variable

(v)   average

(vi)   average fixed

(vii)   total

(viii)   average

29

Quantity	Price	Total revenue	Fixed cost	Variable cost	Total cost	Average fixed cost	Average variable cost	Average total cost	Profit
0	–	–	200	–	200	–	–	–	–
									200
1	180	180	200	50	250	200	50	250	–70
2	170	340	200	100	300	100	50	150	40
3	160	480	200	150	350	66.6	50	116.6	130
4	150	600	200	200	400	50	50	100	200
5	140	700	200	250	450	40	50	90	250
6	130	780	200	300	500	33.3	50	83.33	280
7	120	840	200	350	550	28.5	50	78.5	290
8	110	880	200	400	600	25	50	5	280
9	100	900	200	450	650	22.2	50	72.2	250
10	90	900	200	500	700	20	50	70	200

Quantity	Given
Price	Given
Total revenue (TR)	TR = quantity × price
	TR at 1 = 1 × 180
	so TR at 2 = 2 × 170 and so on.
Fixed cost	Fixed cost = total cost at zero output = 200
Variable cost	Now we have two known variables.
	If fixed cost + variable cost = total cost, then variable cost = total cost — fixed cost, so at output 1: 250 – 200 = 50
Total cost (TC)	Given
Average fixed cost (AFC)	$AFC = \dfrac{\text{fixed cost}}{\text{output}}$
	So at output 1, $AFC = \dfrac{200}{1} = 200$
	At output 10, $\dfrac{200}{10} = 20$
Average variable cost (AVC)	$AVC = \dfrac{\text{variable cost}}{\text{output}}$
	so average variable cost = 500/10 = 50
Average total cost	$\text{Average total cost} = \dfrac{TC}{\text{output}}$
	It can also be calculated by adding the two previous columns AFC + AVC
Profit	Difference between total revenue and total cost
	If TR > TC, then we have profit
	If TC > TR, then we have loss

30   3

Quantity	Price	Total revenue	Total cost	Profit
0	–	–	20	(20)
1	45	45	35	10
2	40	80	45	35
3	35	105	60	45
4	30	120	90	30

THE MARKET SYSTEM AND THE COMPETITIVE PROCESS

CONSUMER BEHAVIOUR AND DEMAND

31

(i) $\dfrac{\% \text{ change in quantity demanded}}{\% \text{ change in price}}$

(ii)   (a)   zero

(b)   zero and – 1

(c)   –1

(d)   –1 and infinity

(e)   infinity

(iii)   1   availability of substitutes

2   proportion of income spent

3   frequency of purchase

4   nature of the good

5   amount of brand loyalty

32

(i)   change in consumers' incomes

(ii)   change in price of substitute good

(iii)   change in price of complementary good

(iv)   change in consumers' tastes

(v)   successful advertising campaign

SUPPLY AND THE MARKET

33

(i) $\dfrac{\%\text{ change in quantity supplied}}{\%\text{ change in price}}$

(ii) 1   the nature of the product

2   availability of other factors

3   government taxation

4   the level of capacity

5   the time scale

34

(i)   an increase in expenditure tax

(ii)   a rise in costs

(iii) a rise in the price of imported raw materials

35

(i)   a government subsidy

(ii)   an increase in technology

(iii) a reduction in the price of imported raw materials

36

The short run is the time it takes to adjust one factor of production and in the long run all factors of production are variable.

PRICE AND OUTPUT DETERMINATION

37

(i)   excess

(ii)   excess

(iii) market equilibrium

38

(i)   It raises the wage above the equilibrium price and thus the demand for labour contracts and the supply of labour extends

(ii)   It could reduce voluntary unemployment since it increases the difference between minimum wage and state benefit

39

Demand and supply of sheep

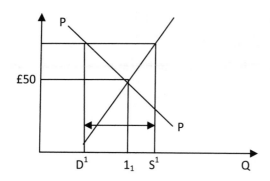

By setting a minimum price above market clearing price, there will be an excess supply ofD1S1.

40

Demand and supply of rented accommodation

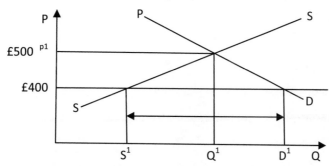

By setting a maximum price below the market clearing price, the government creates an excess demand of S^1D^1.

LARGE SCALE PRODUCTION

41

(i)   minimum efficient scale (MES)

(ii)   economies of scale

(iii)   diseconomies of scale

(iv)   diversification

(v)   merger

(vi)   takeover

(vii)   horizontal

(viii) vertical

(ix)   lateral

(x)   backwards

42

    (i)   Technical economies of scale on production

    (ii)   Managerial economies where functions could becombined, for example accountancy

    (iii)   Trading economies such as bulk buying

    (iv)   Financial economies – should be able to borrow money at lower interest rates

    (v)   Research and Development economies could be achieved

43

    (i)   increasing bureaucracy and loss of control

    (ii)   poorer labour relations

    (iii)   difficulties of communication in a larger business

44

    (i)   *primary* – natural goods

    (ii)   *secondary* – produced goods

    (iii)   *tertiary* – services

45

    (i)   economies of scale

    (ii)   increase market share

    (iii)   fend off competition

46

    (i)   economies of scale

    (ii)   forward to get closer to market

    (iii)   backwards easier access to raw materials

47

    (i)   not solely reliant on one product or industry

    (ii)   functional duties can be shared, for example IT

48

Advantages

    (i)   workers better at job, so greater output

    (ii)   market dictates specialists, for example lawyers

Disadvantages

    (i)   job repetition

    (ii)   specialisation leads to functional divisions within the company

49

    (i)   economy

    (ii)   effectiveness

    (iii)   efficiency

50

    (i)   division of profits – dividends or managers' bonuses

    (ii)   time scale – managers appraised on short-term results

    (iii)   takeovers – higher share price vs redundancy

    (iv)   Annual general meeting (AGM) – re-elect the directors or not

MARKET STRUCTURE

51

    (i)   sole trader

    (ii)   partnership

    (iii)   private limited company

    (iv)   plc

    (v)   takers

    (vi)   homogeneous

    (vii)   excess capacity

    (viii) barriers to entry

    (ix)   excess

    (x)   predatory

52

    (i)   marginal cost — marginal revenue

           profits are maximised

    (ii)   average cost — marginal cost

           average cost is minimised

    (iii)   marginal cost — price

           society welfare is maximised

53

(i)	control of supply	– natural
(ii)	advertising	– artificial
(iii)	high fixed costs	– natural
(iv)	patents	– artificial
(v)	regulation	– artificial
(vi)	Government licences, for example television	– artificial

54

(i) control supply

(ii) identify at least two separate markets, that is, different elasticities of demand

(iii) prevent those who pay lower price from selling to those prepared to pay higher price

55

(i) maximise market share – survival

(ii) maximise revenue – maximise managers' salaries

(iii) satisfices – keep all stakeholders happy

(iv) prevent new firms from entering the market. Spend money on advertising and branding

56

A natural monopoly is one where cost per unit falls as output rises. A consumer might be better off because one firm could produce more cheaply and competition would lead to inefficiency.

57

	Perfect competition	*Monopolistic competition*	*Oligopoly*	*Monopoly*
No. of firms	many	many	few	one
Type of products	homogeneous	slightly differential	differential	one
Price competition	perfect	some	avoided	none
Type of demand curve	perfectly elastic	elastic	inelastic	inelastic
Information	perfect	perfect	imperfect	imperfect
Barriers to entry	none	none	many	impossible to enter
Exists in real life	no	becoming extinct	the norm	where govts. allow

THE PUBLIC SECTOR AND REGULATION

58

Arguments in favour of nationalisation

(i)   natural monopolies such as public utilities

(ii)   sufficient capital available for investment because of government support

(iii) provision of uneconomical services, for example rural transport

(iv)   strategic control over key industries

(v)   protects employment, for example keeping open uneconomic coal mines

(vi)   leads to a more even and fairer distribution of income and wealth

59

Arguments in favour of privatisation

(i)   improved efficiency: many state industries were overmanned

(ii)   privatisation has led to wider share ownership which gives workers better understanding of the profit motive

(iii) competition should lead to better quality and lower prices

(iv)   profits made by privatised firms will provide extra funding to the treasury

(v)   privatisation should lead to greater economic freedom

60

Six criticisms of privatisation

(i)   Many government assets were sold off below their market price. Harold MacMillan described this as 'selling off the family silver'

(ii)   Executives have paid themselves excessive salaries in protected markets

(iii) Public sector monopolies have just been transferred to private sector monopolies

(iv)   Many shares were sold to overseas individuals and institutions, thereby weakening The Balance of Payments

(v)   Fewer services and higher prices, for example rural transport

(vi)   Loss of jobs: in 1993 British Telecom shed 15,000 jobs

61

Public goods are products, such as defence where the consumption by one person does not diminish someone else's (non-rivalry) and that person cannot stop someone else benefiting from it (non-exclusivity).

A merit good is one which left purely to market forces would lead to an underprovision of that good or service, for example education. A merit good is often free to the consumer but it is not a free good, for example primary school education.

62

Many industries in the United Kingdom were privatised and regulated. With public monopolies being transferred to private monopolies, the government accepted the need to create regulatory watchdogs. The role of specific industry regulators (SIRS) is twofold.

(i)   SIRS can introduce an element of competition by setting price caps and performance standards.

(ii)   SIRS can speed up the introduction of competition in such markets by reducing barriers to entry.

THE MACROECONOMIC CONTENT OF BUSINESS: THE DOMESTIC ECONOMY

NATIONAL INCOME

63

(i)   income

(ii)   output

(iii) expenditure

64

(i)   economic planning

(ii)   to see if economy is rising or falling

(iii) to compare its growth rates with other countries

THE CIRCULAR FLOW OF INCOME

65

(i)   interest rates

(ii)   wealth

(iii) taxation policy

(iv)   inflation

(v)   structure of population

66

(i)   assumes firms have no spare capacity

(ii)   assumes firms have funds to finance increase in demand

(iii) assumes investment decisions are based on one year's sales figures

67

	Injections		*Withdrawals*
(i)	investment	(i)	savings
(ii)	government expenditure	(ii)	taxation
(iii)	exports	(iii)	imports

68

current income Y   =£100 million

full employment Y   = £125 million

value of MPC   = 0.8

multiplier $= \dfrac{1}{1-\text{MPC}} = \dfrac{1}{1-0.8} = \dfrac{1}{0.2} = 5$

Therefore government expenditure would need to rise by £5m (× 5) = £25 million

69

The paradox arises since the increase in savings leads to a reduction in consumption and increase leakages from the circular flow of income.

Lower consumption will lead to lower income. Lower income will thus lead to a fall in savings.

70

(i)	recession
(ii)	depression
(iii)	trough
(iv)	recovery
(v)	boom

71

(i)	False
(ii)	True
(iii)	False
(iv)	True
(v)	True
(vi)	True
(vii)	True
(viii)	True

INFLATION AND UNEMPLOYMENT

72

    (i)   Sources of cost push inflation include: rising import prices, increased indirect taxation, rising wages unrelated to the demand for labour

    (ii)   Sources of demand pull inflation include: excessive monetary growth high government expenditure, high consumer expenditure, high investment expenditure and high export demand

73

Gainers		*Losers*	
(i)	Borrowers	(i)	Savers
(ii)	Those with index-linked incomes	(ii)	Those on fixed incomes
(iii)	Those who invest in assets	(iii)	Those who hold cash

74

Quantity theory of money states that MV (the supply of money) — PT (the demand for money) where M is the money supply, V is the velocity of circulation, P is the price level and T is the transactions demand.

75

    (i)   *Seasonal* – where people are not employed all the year round, for example tourism

    (ii)   *Structural* – caused by changes in the structure of an economy where the demand for some goods and services fall, for example coal and steel

    (iii)   *Cyclical* – caused by a downturn in the level of economic activity, that is, the trade cycle

    (iv)   *Frictional unemployment* – where people are in between jobs

    (v)   *Voluntary unemployment* – where people choose not to work for whatever reason

76

    (i)   A lack of demand for goods and services

    (ii)   Where trade unions "price workers out of jobs" by high wage demands

    (iii)   Long term decline of particular industries or occupations

    (iv)   Where state benefits are higher than certain jobs, caused by tax rates in excess of 100%, that is, the poverty trap

    (v)   High real rates of interest which will discourage investment

77

Phillips curve is based on empirical research on the UK economy by LSE professor A. W. Phillips. He suggested that there was an inverse relationship between inflation and unemployment in the economy. This argument lost favour in the 1970s when a number of economies suffered from stagflation (rising prices and rising unemployment) something the Keynesians had no answer to.

78

Supply-side policies include:

(i)   Lower direct taxes: By allowing people to keep more of their income they will work more hours

(ii)   Privatisation: Competition will encourage firms to be more efficient

(iii)   Reduction in state benefits: This should reduce the number of those who are voluntarily unemployed

(iv)   Increase in the amount spent on education and training: This should improve the efficiency of the current and future workforce

(v)   Removal of trade union privileges: Main impact is to reduce the price of labour

(vi)   Competition policy: Reducing anti-competitive behaviour by firms especially those with monopoly power

79

(i)   Loss of tax revenue to the government

(ii)   Loss of output

(iii)   Loss of income to the unemployed

(iv)   Damage to skills and confidence of the unemployed

80

Keynesians believe that unemployment is caused by insufficient demand in the economy, that is, a deflationary gap.

Monetarists believe that unemployment is caused by the supply price being too high.

MONETARY POLICY

81

(i)   M = money supply

(ii)   V = velocity of circulation

(iii)   P = price level

(iv)   T = transactions demand

82

(i)   *Interest rates:* Affect the price at which individuals and institutions can borrow money

(ii)   *Open market operations:* The buying and selling of government securities

(iii)   *Reserve asset ratio:* The proportion of assets banks must hold in liquid format

83

    (i)   Consumer expenditure would fall

    (ii)   The market price of assets would fall

    (iii)   Foreign funds would be attracted to UK financial institutions

    (iv)   The exchange rate would rise

    (v)   Inflation should fall

84

The theoretical basis for the Medium-Term Financial Strategy (MTFS) was that excessive public spending led to budget deficits which in turn raised monetary growth and fuelled demand-pull inflation when supply did not keep pace with this growth.

85

The credit multiplier is found by taking the reciprocal of the reserve asset ratio so

    (i) $1/(1/10)$ = 10

    (ii) $1/(1/5)$ = 5

    (iii) $1/(1/4)$ = 4

    (iv) $1/(4/10)$ = 2.5

    (v) $1/(1/2)$ = 2

86

(i)

Assets		Liabilities	
Loans	£80m	Deposits	£95m
Cash	£15m		
	£95m		£95m

(ii)

Assets		Liabilities	
Loans	£76m	Deposits	£95m
Cash	£19m		
	£95m		£95m

87

Inflation targeting has been in existence since 1997 when the Bank of England was given independence in monetary policy and was given an inflation target of 2.5% by the Chancellor.

88

In the short run an increase in the money supply will increase real output, in the long run it will only increase prices.

90

89

Economic variable	Keynesians	Monetarists
(i) Demand for money	Expressed by the liquidity preference schedules, savings may be held in the form of cash ("idle balances") if interest rates are low and speculators believe that they will rise	Money mainly demanded for transactions. Any portion of income not spent will be saved in an interest-bearing form. Idle balances will not be held
(ii) Supply (stock) of money	Interacts with the speculative demand for money to set interest rates. Additional money entering the system will be accompanied by lower interest rates which will induce spectators to exchange some of their bonds for cash	The quantity theory of money predicts that the money supply is closely connected with the rate of inflation. Additional money entering the system will be spent (as people do not hold idle balances), causing prices to rise
(iii) Interest rates	Set by the interaction of the demand for, and supply of, money	Set by the interaction of the demand for, and supply of, loanable funds investment and savings
(iv) Investment	Influenced by interest rates (compared to the marginal efficiency of capital), but much more strongly by entrepreneurs' animal spirits	Determined primarily by interest rates
(v) Savings	Determined by the level of income, as the residual after the consumption decision is made (using the consumption function)	Determined primarily by interest rates
(vi) Government policy	Control the economy using demand management	Allow market forces to govern. Ensure that markets are as competitive as possible and, by supply growth, prevent inflation from distorting price signals

90

(i) Free from political interference

(ii) Can concentrate on inflation

FISCAL POLICY

91

(i) certainty

(ii) convenience

(iii) equitable

(iv) economy

92

(i) expenditure

(ii) income, wealth

(iii) *ad valorum* tax

(iv) progressive

(v) regressive

(vi) corporation

(vii) social security

(viii) inheritance

(ix) capital gains

(x) customs, excise

93

Advantages

(i) high levels of income tax are a disincentive to work

(ii) individuals have no choice but to pay income tax

(iii) high-tax payers, that is, high-income earners will relocate to low-tax countries.

Disadvantages

(i) it is regressive

(ii) it leads to a more uneven distribution of income and wealth

(iii) it pushes up prices of goods and services without adding to the value.

94

(i)   to ensure that there is an adequate supply of essentials, for example agricultural products

(ii)   to prevent unemployment (iii)to protect producers against unfair foreign competitors

95

(i)   an ageing population

(ii)   a rise in unemployment

(iii)   increased expenditure on health and education

(iv)   political commitments

(v)   inflation

96

Fiscal stance refers to the effect the government budget on aggregate monetary demand in the economy. For example, if government expenditure was above taxation, the stance would be expansionary since this would raise aggregate demand.

97

Monetarists might worry about a large positive PSNCR for two reasons:

(i)   It either expands the money supply with inflationary pressures or

(ii)   It raises interest rates, thereby crowding out private sector investment

98

The PSNCR is the actual public sector borrowing requirement (PSBR) over a fiscal year. The national debt is the accumulated government debt which goes back to the 17th century and the setting up of the Bank of England.

99

If national income is rising over time, in real terms the absolute amount falls. Governments are more concerned about being able to finance such a deficit. It is the same for an individual. For someone earning in excess of £100,000 per annum, a £10,000 overdraft interest is not a major problem. For someone earning £10,000 per annum, it represents 100% of their actual salary and they do have a problem.

GOVERNMENT ECONOMIC POLICY

100

(i)   full employment

(ii)   stable prices

(iii)   economic growth

(iv)   balance of payments

101

    (i)   fiscal policy

    (ii)   monetary policy

    (iii)   supply-side policy

    (iv)   exchange rate policy

102

    (i)   monetarism

    (ii)   increase training and education

    (iii)   privatisation

    (iv)   reduce direct taxation

103

    (i)   lower interest rates to encourage investment

    (ii)   increase capital allowances to encourage investment

    (iii)   encourage the sharing of technology amongst firms

    (iv)   lower exchange rates to promote exports

104

    (i)   to reduce unemployment

    (ii)   to protect from unfair competition

    (iii)   to help run a loss-making service that would not be provided, if left to market forces, for example rural transport

105

Marketable debt is any debt which is tradeable in the financial markets, for example treasury bills.

Non-marketable debts which the government issues are in the form of national savings products, such as national savings certificates or premium savings bonds.

106

    (i)   based on inaccurate information

    (ii)   based on out-of-date information

    (iii)   based on political rather than economic reasons (iv)   time lag it takes for policies to make their mark

107

 (i) lack of business optimism

 (ii) lack of consumer optimism

 (iii) events in the rest of the world (iv)   inappropriate government policies

108

Fiscal drag happens during periods of inflation where incomes are pushed into higher tax brackets resulting in a fall in real disposable income.

109

 (i)   monetarist

 (ii)   monetarist

 (iii) Keynesian

 (iv) Keynesian

 (v)   monetarist

 (vi) Keynesian

 (vii) monetarist

THE MACROECONOMIC CONTEXT OF BUSINESS: THE INTERNATIONAL ECONOMY

GLOBALISATION AND TRADE

110

 (i) greater choice of products and services

 (ii) greater competition between firms and nations

 (iii) economies of scale

 (iv) specialisation allowing countries to develop greater skills

111

Country X has an absolute advantage over country Y in producing a good and it can do so using fewer resources.

Country X has a comparative advantage over country Y in producing a good when they have a lower opportunity cost of producing that good than country Y.

112

    (i)   to protect balance of payments

    (ii)   to protect domestic employment

    (iii)   to protect infant industries

    (iv)   for strategic reasons, for example agriculture and defence

113

    (i)   *Tariffs* – taxes on imports

    (ii)   *Quotas* – restrictions on imports

    (iii)   *Export subsidies* – subsidies on exports

    (iv)   *Exchange controls* – quotas on currency

114

A multinational corporation is a company engaged in production facilities outside their country of origin.

115

    (i)   consumer choice is reduced

    (ii)   less competition between firms and nations

    (iii)   lower world economic welfare

116

    (i)   An increase in economic welfare as capital is transferred to economies where rates of return are higher

    (ii)   Promotes technological transfer

    (iii)   Creates employment

    (iv)   Should improve balance of payments of recipient country

117

    (i)   *Factor immobility* – unlike the model of perfect competition, factors of production do not move freely

    (ii)   *Transport costs* – on bulky low value goods, there will be no advantage of specialisation and trade

    (iii)   *The size of the market* – may not be big enough or ready for certain products and services

    (iv)   *Government policies* – for reasons suggested in Question 20.3, governments may wish to discourage free trade

BALANCE OF PAYMENTS

118

- (i) visible
- (ii) invisible
- (iii) current
- (iv) financial
- (v) balancing item, statistical error

119

- (i) −£2 million (10 − 12)
- (ii) +£1 million (6 − 5)
- (iii) −£2 million + £1 million + £500,000 = −£500,000

120

- (i) Visible earnings are our exports on tangible goods such as cars, textiles and foodstuffs
- (ii) Invisible trade is trade in services such as shipping, banking and insurance
- (iii) A current account deficit is where a combination of the visible and invisible balance is negative
- (iv) Since the balance of payments as a whole always balances to zero any apparent imbalance must be due to errors and omissions in the accounts. Thus a figure that balances the accounts to zero is entered under this heading

121

Hot money is not stolen money! It is money which moves from one capital centre to the next if the owners can achieve a higher rate of return elsewhere.

122

- (i) airlines
- (ii) insurance
- (iii) banking

123

- (i) 10,799 deficit
- (ii) 10,672 deficit
- (iii) 2,183 deficit

124

Deindustrialisation is the absolute loss of jobs in the manufacturing sector of an economy. It has also been described as a country's inability to maintain full employment and a balance of payments equilibrium.

125

(i)   *Devaluation* – makes exports cheaper and imports more expensive

(ii)   *Tariffs* – make imports more expensive

(iii) *Quotas* – restrict imports

(iv)   *Export subsidies* – give subsidies to export-producing industries

126

Governments are reluctant to use deflation to solve a balance of payments problem because deflationary policies are unpopular because they lead to reduced spending and unemployment. In a democracy that is no way for governments to be re-elected.

THE FINANCIAL SYSTEM

THE FINANCIAL SYSTEM

127

(i)   transactions demand

(ii)   precautionary demand

(iii) speculative demand

128

(i)   income

(ii)   nature of the individual

(iii) interest rates

129

(i)   £100 because I would get the same yield by putting the money in a bank account

(ii)   Fall because the bond now becomes a less attractive investment in relation to others

(iii) Rise because the bond now becomes a more attractive investment in relation to others

(iv)   It is a question of equalising the yields so if interest rates are 5%, this would give us a 5% yield on a bond if we paid £200 for it

(v)   As in (iv) we would get a yield of 20% if we paid £50 for the bond. If we bought 2 for £100 this would give us a yield of £20 or 20%

(vi)   Always at face value £100

130

    (i)   length of the loan

    (ii)   risk of the loan

    (iii)   size of the loan

    (iv)   rate of return required by lender

    (v)   level of competition in the money market

131

    (i)   Base rate is the standard rate from which all bank lending rates are set

    (ii)   It is the rate a bank will pay someone, holding a deposit account, who wants to be able to withdraw money at any time

    (iii)   It is the rate a bank will pay someone, holding a deposit account, who must wait for 3 months before they can withdraw any money from that account

    (iv)   The mortgage rate is the rate at which building societies will lend money to individuals who wish to borrow money to purchase property

    (v)   With 90-day access, lenders have access to your funds for an extra 90 days which they can invest at a higher rate

    (vi)   Base rate is never the rate at which banks lend, for personal overdrafts they normally charge about 5% above the base rate which is higher than the mortgage rate

    (vii) The rate of inflation

    (viii) 4.5%

132

    A   cut

    B   buy

    C   reduced

133

    (i)   *Expectations theory:* Investors expect interest rates to rise in the future

    (ii)   *Liquidity preference theory:* Investors have a natural preference for holding cash, therefore must be compensated for being deprived of their cash

    (iii)   *Market segment theory:* There are different types of investors who are interested in different segments of the curve, for example banks will invest at the short end while pension funds will invest at the longer end of the scale

134

(i)   False

(ii)   True

(iii)   True

(iv)   True

(v)   True

(vi)   False

(vii)   True

(viii) False

(ix)   True

135

(i)   it must be widely acceptable

(ii)   it must have a high value weight ratio

(iii)   it must be divisible to settle debts of different denominations

(iv)   it must not be easily produced, counterfeited or debased in value

136

(i)   Pension funds

(ii)   Insurance companies

(iii)   Unit trusts

(iv)   Investment trusts

(v)   Fund managers

137

(i)   Gilt-edged

(ii)   UK fully listed securities

(iii)   Alternative Investment Market (AIM)

(iv)   Overseas securities

138

(i)   Financial Times Stock Exchange Index

(ii)   Gilt-Edged Market Markers

(iii)   Stock Exchange Automated Quotation System

(iv)   A computerised system giving access to different information systems, for example SEAQ

(v)   The computer system which records the holdings of securities and the settlements of traders

(vi)   Stock Exchange Daily Official List

(vii)   Alternative Investment Market

(viii) Unlisted Securities Market

(ix)   London Inter Bank Bid Rate

(x)   London Inter Bank Offer Rate

139

(i)   advice on takeover and mergers

(ii)   advice on raising capital

(iii)   act as an issuing house

(iv)   underwrites new issues

(v)   issue Eurobonds

(vi)   provide fund management

140

(i)   The building societies are still prevalent in house purchase mortgages

(ii)   The building society deposits and loans tend to be for smaller amounts

(iii)   The building societies still tend to lend long-term and not get involved in the money market

141

(i)   They are a company

(ii)   They are listed on the stock exchange

(iii)   They have equity and debt capital

(iv)   They invest in the shares of other companies

(v)   They provide an opportunity for small investors to diversify their investment

142

    (i)   They are a trust in the legal sense

    (ii)   Money raised comes only from investors

    (iii)   The Securities and Investment Board only allow unit trusts to undertake in certain investments

143

    (i)   Investment Trusts

    (ii)   Merchant Banks

    (iii)   Local authorities

    (iv)   Regional Enterprise Boards

    (v)   Industrial and Commercial Finance Corporation

144

    (i)   Ordinary shares

    (ii)   Preference shares

    (iii)   Debentures

    (iv)   Convertible stocks

    (v)   Derivatives

145

    (i)   Dow Jones

    (ii)   Nikkei

    (iii)   Discount

    (iv)   Sterling interbank

    (v)   Eurocurrency

    (vi)   Commercial paper

    (vii) Parallel

    (viii) Bill of exchange

    (ix)   Bankers' acceptance

    (x)   Eligible bill

FOREIGN EXCHANGE

146

    (i)   overvalued

    (ii)   buy

    (iii)   Q2–Q3

    (iv) $2 = £1

147

    (i)   Monetary policy becomes more effective

    (ii)   Automatic adjustment to balance of payments surplus or deficit

    (iii)   Exchange rate becomes instrument not objective of policy

148

    (i)   Uncertainty makes trade more difficult

    (ii)   Fiscal policy becomes ineffective

    (iii)   Depreciation on its own may not correct a deficit

149

A managed or dirty float is where a government allows the market to dictate exchange rates on a day-to-day basis but governments will intervene if they think exchange rate is too high or too low.

150

The purchasing power parity theory states that the value of an exchange rate should reflect what that currency can buy, for example if a Big Mac costs $2 in New York and the exchange rate is $2 – £1 then a Big Mac in London should cost £1.

151

    (i)   relative inflation rates

    (ii)   trade flows

    (iii)   investment flows

    (iv)   economic prospects

    (v)   speculator's judgement

    (vi)   technical analysis

152

    (i)   Inflation should be within 1.5 percentage points of the average of the three best performing members for a period of one year

    (ii)   Government deficits should not exceed 3 per cent of GDP

    (iii) A 2.25% narrow band for their currency, without initiating a realignment for at least two years

    (iv) Long-term interest rates must be within 2 percentage points of the three best performing states, in terms of price stability

153

    (iii)   True

    (iv)   False

    (v)   True

    (vi)   True

    (vii)   False

    (viii) True

    (ix)   False

    (x)   True

Section 4

ANSWERS TO OBJECTIVE TEST QUESTIONS

THE GOALS AND DECISIONS OF ORGANISATIONS

SCARCE RESOURCES

1   C

In a market economy, producers in the search of profits must respond to consumer demand. Thus the allocation of resources reflects consumer preferences as expressed in their expenditure.

2   C

Mixed economy.

3   D

A market economy does not provide an even distribution of income and wealth.

4   D

The NHS – because this is a merit good.

5   B

A fall in population will reduce a country's productive capacity.

6   C

Gross national product per head.

THE BUSINESS ORGANISATION

7   FALSE

False is the correct answer because some organisations have other motives that are not linked to profits, e.g. charities.

8   A

A is the correct answer because the other organisations are normally found in the private sector.

9   C

C is the correct answer because this is the main activity in the public sector. Options A and B relate to the private sector and D to a mutual organisation.

10   PRINCIPAL

Principal is the correct answer because directors make decisions on behalf of the shareholders (the principal).

11   D

A company which operates a policy of satisficing is trying to keep everybody concerned happy.

12   D

Health and education are examples of merit goods since they are available to the consumer below market price. Road congestion is an example of a social cost.

13   C

Not-for-profit organisations can be found in both sectors, for example private sector charity and public sector local authority.

SHAREHOLDER WEALTH

14   D

Dividend	$\dfrac{12}{120}$	10%
Capital gain	$\dfrac{30}{120}$	$\dfrac{25\%}{35\%}$

15   C

$$\frac{8.6}{204} \times 100 = 4.2\%$$

16   D

$$EPS = \frac{£15,000}{70,000} \times 100 = 21.4$$

17 D

$$\frac{£10,000}{(1.1)^4} = £6,830$$

18 B

Share prices are likely to fall because an increase in interest will raise borrowing costs which will affect profit.

19 C

At the end of the period the amount owed would be

£100 × (1 + 0.035)^{12} = £151.11

of which £51.11 is interest.

20 A

A is the correct answer because this measure shows that the company is maximising short-run profit in relation to assets to increase shareholder wealth. Net present value is related to investment which measures long run increases in shareholder wealth.

21 FALSE

False is the correct answer because Earnings Per Share is measured using profit after interest and tax.

22 C

C is the correct answer because this relates to an increase in shareholder wealth in the long run. The other measures are relevant when measuring short-run shareholder value.

23 C

C is the correct answer because EPS shows what each share can earn, not how shareholder value will actually increase.

24 B

B is the correct answer using the calculation shown below:

Timing	0	1	2	3
Cash flow (£000)	(200)	750	500	(300)
Discount factor	1	0.909	0.826	0.751
Cash flow	(200)	682.75	413.00	(225.3)

25 D

D is the correct answer because:

PV = 2,000 × 1 + 2,000 × 6.247 = £14,494 (nearest £)

26   B

B is the correct answer because the perpetuity literally continues forever (it is perpetual).

27   B

B is the correct answer because NPV shows the potential increase in shareholder wealth, in cash terms. Shareholders have a preference for cash over profits, as this directly increases their wealth.

28   C

C is the correct answer because the discount factor to use is .909, multiplied by the £1,000 gives £909.

CORPORATE GOVERNANCE

29   A

Directors are appointed by shareholders.

30   A

The non-executive director is appointed by the executive directors.

31   D

Directors practising insider dealing is not an advantage since it is illegal.

32   C

C is the correct answer because other options normally erode shareholder value; maximising cash flows improves shareholder value.

33   A

A is the correct answer because, although improving employee welfare is important, this is not seen as a primary objective of corporate governance.

34   C

C is the correct answer because this should be the role of stakeholders.

35   TRUE

True is the correct answer because good governance enables companies to improve their credit ratings, thus improving access to forms of capital.

36   FALSE

False is the correct answer because these roles are normally split to avoid too much power being given to one person.

COST BEHAVIOUR AND PRICING DECISIONS

37   **A**

Average fixed cost = $\dfrac{\text{Fixed cost}}{Q}$

Fixed cost = Total cost at zero

so $\dfrac{£100}{5}$ = £20

38   **A**

Diminishing returns occur in the short run because one factor of production is fixed.

39   **A**

Diseconomies of scale occur when long run average costs begin to rise.

40   **B**

Total costs and total variable costs will rise, fixed costs will remain constant, average costs could rise or fall.

41   **D**

A business which satisfices will try to achieve a target which is acceptable to all parties.

42   **B**

A function of profit is a signal to producers not consumers.

43   **D**

If a firm is enjoying economies of scale, then unit cost is falling as output rises.

44   **C**

C is the correct answer because output has increased in percentage terms by more than the increase in inputs.

45   **TRUE**

True is the correct answer because long-run costs fall initially as the company obtains economies of scale.

46   **DISECONOMIES**

Diseconomies is the correct answer because in the long-run average costs increase.

47   B

B is the correct answer because diseconomies of scale cause the long-term average cost curve to rise. Diminishing marginal returns cause the short-term average cost curve to rise.

48   B

B is the correct answer because the other options are external economies of scale (including D which refers to provision of skilled labour to the company, not the training of labour within the company).

THE MARKET SYSTEM AND THE COMPETITIVE PROCESS

CONSUMER BEHAVIOUR AND DEMAND

49   B

Elasticity of demand

$$= \frac{\% \text{ change in quantity demanded}}{\% \text{ change in price}}$$

$$= \frac{+25\%}{-20\%} = -1.25$$

50   D

The price of the good itself is not held constant when we draw the demand curve.

51   D

If total expenditure remains the same we have unitary elasticity.

52   B

B is the correct answer because demand measures the quantity of a product that consumers will purchase at different price levels. Only the price of the product is allowed to vary to construct a demand curve.

53   C

C is the correct answer because it shows a movement along a demand curve; supply is unaffected (in fact no supply curve is shown).

54   B

B is the correct answer because this is the effect derived from the theory of diminishing marginal utility.

55   D

D is the correct answer because this is the definition of a complementary good.

56   B

B is the correct answer because an increase in income normally results in an increase in demand.

57   D

D is the correct answer because technological progress increases the efficiency of production and lowers costs.

SUPPLY AND THE MARKET

58   A

Regardless of the level of taxation, the profit maximisation level remains the same, just 10% less, so leave price and output the same.

59   D

In the short run, a firm can continue to operate provided they can cover variable costs.

60   B

A government subsidy, an increase in technology and lower input prices would all shift the supply curve to the right, a government expenditure tax would shift to the left.

61   D

$$\text{Elasticity of supply} = \frac{\% \text{ change in quantity supplied}}{\% \text{ change in price}}$$

so $\dfrac{+20\%}{+10\%} = +2$

PRICE AND OUTPUT DETERMINATION

62   C

The supply of agricultural products in the short run is inelastic.

63   A

This will lead to excess demand.

64   C

A system of quotas was introduced to reduce supply.

65   D

D is the correct answer because there is currently excess supply in the market; customers must be encouraged to purchase more of the good. The supplier needs to attract more demand – this can be done by decreasing price.

66   B

B is the correct answer because an increase in income will result in an overall increase in demand at all price levels.

67   D

D is the correct answer because manufacturing/supply becomes more efficient, thus moving the supply curve to the right.

68   B

B is the correct answer because the cost of supply will increase, moving the supply curve upwards and to the left; demand is unchanged.

LARGE SCALE PRODUCTION

69   B

If Tesco plc acquired a food processing company, this would be an example of vertical integration backwards.

70   D

By reducing entry costs, this allows more firms into the market which is not a strategic argument for horizontal integration.

71   D

Low fixed costs will encourage more firms to enter a market, thereby increasing competition within an industry.

72   D

Technical, financial, trading and managerial are all examples of internal economies of scale.

73   C

The Monopolies and Mergers Commission/Competition Commission was set up to see how public interest was affected where one firm or more controlled the market.

MARKET STRUCTURE

74   C

Branding is the only barrier to entry of the alternatives offered.

75   C

An artificial barrier is one created by government – an example being the issue of patents.

76   D

Alternatives (iii) and (iv) are examples of price discrimination because the products or services are the same, alternatives (i) and (ii) are selling different products and services.

77   B

A natural monopoly may be beneficial to the consumer because the company can obtain economies of scale.

78   D

Extensive advertising is not an example of anti-competitive behaviour by large firms.

79   FALSE

False is the correct answer because the government can also establish monopolies (e.g. supply of utilities or the granting of a patent).

80   FALSE

False is the correct answer because the public sector relates to the government – where the profit motive is not always relevant.

81   D

D is the correct answer because production could be increased to lower costs.

82   C

C is the correct answer because there is normally some barrier to entry such as lack of specific resources.

THE PUBLIC SECTOR AND REGULATION

83   A

A pure public good is one which no individual can be excluded from consuming it.

84   A

If a chemical company has reduced the level of pollution from its factory, this will lead to a fall in social costs.

85   C

Health and education are examples of merit goods. Defence is a public good and water is a necessity.

86   C

A good which is characterised by both rivalry and excludability is known as a private good.

87   B

Privatisation will lead to a less even distribution of income and wealth.

88   D

Bread is a necessity consumed by everyone but it is not produced by the state.

89   A

When privatisation took place in the United Kingdom, assets were transferred from the public sector and money went to the government.

90   A

If the production of a good results in a positive externality, the government should give the producer a subsidy which reflects the marginal benefit from the consumption of the good.

91   C

The government may discourage horizontal mergers in manufacturing industry because consumers may lose out if the merged firm acquires market dominance.

92   A

A is the correct answer because the resulting theory looks like a 'cobweb' on supply and demand curves.

93   C

C is the correct answer because although tax rates can be determined easily, the revenue obtained may fluctuate.

94   D

D is the correct answer because this action will not help producers determine how much of the good to supply.

95   FALSE

False is the correct answer because a set-aside payment is the amount given to a supplier to take resources out of production and so reduce supply.

96   D

D is the correct answer because the lead time to amend the supply of wheat in response to changes in prices is one year.

THE MACROECONOMIC CONTENT OF BUSINESS: THE DOMESTIC ECONOMY

NATIONAL INCOME

97   A

The existence of the hidden economy and voluntary labour would underestimate the real value of goods and services.

98   D

A transfer payment is an income received for which there is no corresponding output, so odd one out is D.

99   D

Double counting can appear on the output side, since the output of one industry may be the input of another.

100   C

Two methods can be used here.

Take the value added at each stage which is the output method or the value of the final product sold, so 1,000 × £1 = £1,000.

101   C

GDP at market prices are normally higher than GDP at factor cost because taxes are normally higher than subsidies.

THE CIRCULAR FLOW OF INCOME

102   B

The sum of the marginal propensity to consume and the marginal propensity to save must be equal to one.

103 D

Taxation is a withdrawal from the circular flow of income.

104 B

Injections	Withdrawals
£m	£m
432	176
249	503
329	298
1,010	977

Since injections are higher than withdrawals, the national income of the economy will start to rise.

105 B

The acceleration principle states that the level of investment varies directly with the rate of change of output.

106 B

National income is in equilibrium where planned injections – planned withdrawals.

107 C

Value of MPC = $\dfrac{\Delta C}{\Delta Y} = \dfrac{15}{20} = 0.75$

108 A

Income needs to rise by £20 million

Value of multiplier = $\dfrac{1}{1-MPC} = \dfrac{1}{MPS} = \dfrac{1}{1-0.8} = \dfrac{1}{0.2} = 5$

So to achieve full employment, investment must rise by x × 5 to make £20 million x = £4 million.

INFLATION AND UNEMPLOYMENT

109 C

Monetarists believe that inflation is caused by governments allowing the money supply to rise at a faster rate than productivity.

110 C

A deflationary gap exists where planned expenditure is below the full employment level of output or income.

111 A

The original Phillips curve suggests that there is an inverse relationship between the rate of inflation and the level of unemployment.

112 D

The gainers from inflation are those who have index-linked incomes and those who invest in non-financial assets.

113 A

The real rate of interest – money rate of interest – rate of inflation

So 5% – 7% = –2%

114 D

A downturn in the level of economic activity is associated with the trade cycle.

115 C

A reduction in demand for any individual good, service or industry is associated with structural unemployment.

116 B

This is a test on the quantity theory of money so MV – PT

PT = £12.50 × 10,000   = 125,000

MV = ? × 10   = 125,000

12,500 × 10   = 125,000

So M is equal to 12,500

117 B

The poverty trap exists because at the lowest level of income the marginal rate of tax is above 100%, that is, individuals become worse off by taking a job.

MONETARY POLICY

118 A

A reduction in the money supply would lead to a fall in the rate of inflation, a rise in the exchange rate and a rise in interest rates.

119 B

MV   = PT

£25 million × V = 100 × 500,000 = £50 million

£25 million × 2 = £50 million so V = 2

120 A

If the government were to pursue a contractionary monetary policy they would raise interest rates so we can eliminate alternatives B and D.

They would sell securities which would be bought by cheques from the banking sector, thereby eliminating banking liquidity.

121 C

An increase in the reserve asset ratio would reduce the level of liquidity in the banking sector.

122 D

Money is all of the following except a hedge against inflation.

123 B

If the Bank of England imposes a restriction on lending to property developers, this is an example of special directives.

124 C

A falling or inverse yield curve implies that interest rates are expected to fall which is why 20 year rate is below 3 year rate.

FISCAL POLICY

125 D

Alternatives A, B and C are policies designed to correct a PSBR whereas an issue of government savings certificates could be used to finance it.

126 D

A progressive tax is one where the tax payment rises at a faster rate than income increases.

127 D

The Public Sector Net Cash Requirement is best described as the amount borrowed by the government and public authorities in a given period.

128 B

The burden of an indirect tax on a good will fall more heavily on a consumer when the demand for a good is inelastic. That is why governments tax goods such as petrol and cigarettes.

129 C

An expansionary fiscal policy involves reducing taxes and increasing expenditure, that is, reducing a withdrawal and increasing an injection.

130 D

VAT, Customs and Excise Duties are expenditure taxes, national insurance is an income tax.

131 C

The four canons of taxation are certainty, convenience, equitable and economy so odd one out is objectivity.

132 D

Alternatives A, B and C are all valid reasons why a government should have a budget deficit. A fall in unemployment should increase government revenue and reduce government expenditure.

133 C

The monetarists would argue that higher economic growth would not follow an increase in government borrowing.

GOVERNMENT ECONOMIC POLICY

134 B

An even distribution may be desirable but it is not a current economic objective.

135 C

Supply-side policy is concerned with shifting the supply curve to the right, increasing unemployment benefit would have the opposite effect.

136 A

Treasury bills and gilt-edged stocks are examples of government marketable debt, national savings certificates are examples of non-marketable debt.

137 C

A reduction in employers' national insurance contributions would be expected to reduce the level of unemployment since it reduces the price of labour.

138 A

A television licence is an example of a regressive tax since a poor person is paying a larger share of his/her income than a rich person.

139 B

Total yield will be high when both demand and supply are inelastic since it will have big impact on price rise and small impact on quantity sold.

140 D

If consumer expenditure rises there will be less money in the long run available for investment.

141 B

Governments wish to control inflation because it damages international competitiveness.

142 B

If governments were seeking to reduce unemployment, they should reduce interest rates and lower taxes.

143 C

People who are prepared to work for below the minimum wage may be prevented from doing so if there is a minimum wage because the supply of labour is being restricted. We are talking about the economic argument here not the moral one.

GLOBALISATION AND TRADE

144 C

The theory of comparative advantage states that a country can benefit from trade even if they have an absolute disadvantage in all commodities.

145 B

Alternatives A, C and D are all examples of protectionism. A fixed exchange rate is a type of exchange rate.

146 B

A country imposes tariffs on foreign goods to protect employment at home.

147 D

A customs union is a free trade area within a certain group of countries who have a common tariff with the rest of the world.

148 D

An increase in the international mobility of factors of production leads to decreasing differences in factor prices between countries.

149 B

A multinational company is best described as one which produces goods and services in more than one country.

150 D

Alternatives A, B and C are all correct. Statement D is half correct, increased competition should lead to lower prices.

151 B

Country B has an absolute advantage in the production of good x so we can eliminate alternatives A and D.

However, country B does not have an absolute advantage in the production of good y so we can eliminate C.

Therefore, by process of elimination, the answer is B.

BALANCE OF PAYMENTS

152 C

If the elasticity of demand for British exports is −2, then a devaluation of sterling should lead to an increase in the total foreign currency expenditure on British goods.

153 A

Tangible exports	£35,432
Tangible imports	£36,607

$$= -£1,175$$

154 D

The balance of payments must always balance. Even if there is a balance of payments deficit, there is a balance for official financing.

155 C

Profits from France	+£5 million
Investment in France	−£10 million
Outflow of	£5 million

156 D

A is a visible transaction

B is an invisible transaction

C is an invisible transaction

D is a capital flow

157 B

A balance of payments deficit is least likely to be corrected by increasing the value of sterling.

THE FINANCIAL SYSTEM

THE FINANCIAL SYSTEM

158 C

Transactions demand is a function of income and wealth.

Precautionary demand is down to the individual.

Speculative demand is a function of different interest rates.

159 B

If the central bank pursues an expansionary open market operations policy it will buy securities from the public who will in turn hold the money with the banking sector, thus increasing the liquidity of the banking sector.

160 B

The bank is making a rate of return of just over 4% over a period of 3 months but interest rates are based on an annual figure giving a return of just over 16%.

161 C

A customer's deposit account is an asset of the customer so is a liability to a clearing bank.

162 B

Transactions demand is determined by consumers' income.

163 A

The crowding out effect is caused by a rise in interest rates as the public sector competes with the private sector for funds, thus reducing private sector investment.

164 D

Credit multiplier = 1/RAR = 1/25% = 4   4 × £100 = £400

165 A

If the market rate of interest falls, the price of bonds will rise because they become a more attractive investment in relation to others.

166 D

D is the correct answer because this relates to the time period over which money is lent or borrowed.

167 B

B is the correct answer because the costs of finding borrowers/lenders with corresponding requirements can be high.

168 AGGREGATION

Aggregation is the correct answer because this accurately describes the process of pooling many small deposits.

169 A

A is the correct answer because the service provided is risk reduction.

170 A

A is the correct answer because B and D are both reasons for longer term savings.

171 FALSE

False is the correct answer because short-term differences between receipts and payments are normally managed using a bank account.

172 D

D is the correct answer because the company will have to increase its stock levels during the year to satisfy demand when its products can be sold.

173 FALSE

False is the correct answer because many items of government expenditure occur frequently e.g. payment of wages, but income occurs less frequently e.g. collection of council tax twice a year.

174 A

A is the correct answer because liquidity looks at how easy it is to sell an asset to release the funds tied up in the asset.

175 C

C is the correct answer because money is in limited supply.

176 C

C is the correct answer because the money market has instruments maturing in less than one year while capital markets have instruments maturing in more than one year.

177 C

C is the correct answer because a bill of exchange is a short-term deposit maturing in less than one year.

178 ORDINARY

Ordinary is the correct answer because these shares provide voting rights indicating ownership of the company.

179 B

B is the correct answer because dividend rates can vary (A), they are not normally repurchased by the company (C) and can only be sold easily for quoted companies (D).

180 FALSE

False is the correct answer because bonds are normally issued at a discount, not a premium.

181 C

C is the correct answer because the nominal value shows the final redemption value e.g. £100.

182 TRUE

True is the correct answer because this is an accurate explanation of a certificate of deposit.

183 CREDIT AGREEMENT

Credit agreement is the correct answer because this is the contract explained in the question.

184 D

D is the correct answer because a mortgage cannot be sold although it can be repaid early.

185 A

A is the correct answer because bills of exchange normally have guarantors (banks) (B), they are short term (3 to 6 months) (C) and can be resold (D).

186 D

You can buy and sell shares through the Stock Exchange but they do not actually engage in the market themselves.

187 D

This question is testing candidates ability to distinguish between short-term money markets and long-term capital markets. Capital markets – A, B and C Money market – Discount houses.

188 A

People or institutions who put their money into high-risk equity finance projects are known as venture capitalists.

189 A

Eurocredit and Eurocurrency are short-term capital markets. The Stock Exchange is primarily domestic capital.

190 C

Debentures, preference shares and convertible stocks are all examples of long-term capital. Factoring is where a company sells part or all of its debtors to a third party. This is regarded as working capital.

FOREIGN EXCHANGE

191 B

The main advantage of a system of flexible or floating exchange rates is that it provides automatic correction of balance of payments.

192 A

Providing finance for countries with a balance of payments deficit is not a function of GATT.

193 B

A devaluation of the exchange rate for a country's currency will normally result in a reduction in the current account deficit and an increase in the level of economic activity.

194 B

A single currency does not necessarily ensure lower interest rates.

195 B

A rise in American interest rates is likely to make funds flow from the UK to the United States which would lead to a fall in the value of sterling.

196 B

If sterling equals £1 to $1.50 a £100,000 car would be $150,000. A reduction in sterling to £1 = $1.40 would reduce the dollar price by $10,000 to $140,000.

197 A

The major disadvantage of a single currency to an individual country is loss of monetary control.

198 D

The least mobile factor of production with regard to mobility within Europe is unskilled labour.

199 D

The only advantage of fixed exchange rates listed here is that fiscal policy is more effective.

200 B

B is the correct answer because this will affect the supply of money as UK residents sell sterling to obtain foreign currencies.

Section 5

MOCK ASSESSMENT 1

1 **The following financial data refers to a company.**

Capital employed	1.1.06	$900,000
Capital employed	31.12.06	$1,100,000
Gross profits for year ending	31.12.06	$105,000
Interest payments year ending	31.12.06	$20,000
Tax paid on profits year ending	31.12.06	$15,000

What is the value of the rate of return on capital for this company? **(2 marks)**

2 **All of the following are essential features of a market economy EXCEPT which ONE?**

A   Private ownership of productive resources

B   Allocation of resources by the price mechanism

C   Absence of entry and exit barriers to and from industries

D   Prices determined by market forces **(2 marks)**

3 **Consider the following data for a proposed investment project.**

Capital cost of the project	$7,000
Life of the investment	3 years
Scrap value of the capital at end of Year 3	$500
Income generated by the project	
Year 1	$2,000
Year 2	$3,000
Year 3	$2,000

From this data you are required to calculate:

(a)   The net present value for the project assuming a discount rate of 10% **(2 marks)**

(b)   Is this project profitable for the company?   yes/no **(1 mark)**

(c)   The net present value for the project assuming a discount rate of 6% and a final scrap value of $1,000 **(2 marks)**

4   All of the following would be expected to raise share values EXCEPT which one?

A   An announcement of higher than expected profits

B   A reduction in corporation tax

C   A rise in interest rates

D   A rise in share prices on overseas stock markets   **(2 marks)**

5   The ... (i) .... in a company are all those who have an interest in the strategy and behaviour of the.. . (ii) .... Their interest may not always coincide with those of the .. . (iii)   .... who are principally interested in ... (iv) .... The task of .... (v) .... is to attempt to reconcile these conflicting interests.

Read the above passage and indicate where each of the following words should be placed in the passage.

A   Management

B   Shareholders

C   Stakeholders

D   Company

E   Profits   **(5 marks)**

6   The principal—agent problem refers to:

A   situations where a company's selling agents are not meeting the company's main sales targets

B   problems arising when a principal delegates authority to an agent but cannot ensure the agent will always act in his/her interest

C   cases where companies lack knowledge on particular markets and have to seek agents to act on their behalf

D   the power a large company may exert over supplier's when it is the dominant buyer of that supplier's output   **(2 marks)**

7   For each of the following economic processes, indicate whether the effect on the *short run average cost* for a firm would be to raise the cost curve, lower the cost curve or to leave the cost curve unaffected.

Economic process	Raise curve	Lower curve	Leave curve unaffected
A rise in wage costs			
Increase opportunities for economies of scale.			
A fall in the price of raw materials			
A shift in the demand curve to the left			

                                                                                (4 marks)

8   Indicate whether each of the following statements is *true* or *false*.

Statement	True	False
The law of diminishing returns shows how long run cost tends to rise if the scale of output becomes too great		
A firm's short run cost curve is always U shaped; the long cost curve may or may not be		
For most firms technological change is one of the most important economies of scale		
Economies of scale act as barrier to entry to industries		

(4 marks)

9   Indicate whether each of the following are typical characteristics of an oligopoly market (yes/no).

Characteristic	Yes	No
A large number of small firms		
A preference for non-price competition over price competition		
Interdependence of decision making		
Ease of entry and exit to and from the industry		

(4 marks)

10   State whether each of the following statements is true or false.

Statement	True	False
Collusion is more likely in oligopoly markets than in other markets		
If there are economies of scale, a monopoly firm may charge lower prices than equivalent firms facing competition		
Oligopolistic firms can never achieve lower long run costs than could competitive firms in the same industry		
Oligopolistic firms can make excess profits but only in the short run		

(4 marks)

11   If a business currently sells 10,000 units of its product per month at $10 per unit and the demand for its product has a price elasticity of –2.5, a rise in the price of the product to $11 will:

A   raise total revenue by $7,250

B   reduce total revenue by $17,500

C   reduce total revenue by $25,000

D   raise total revenue by $37,500   **(2 marks)**

12 Which ONE of the following is a natural barrier to the entry of new firms into an industry?

    A   Large initial capital costs

    B   The issuing of patents

    C   A government awarded franchise

    D   The licensing of professions   **(2 marks)**

13 The following data refers to an industry consisting of 6 companies.

Company	Sales	Market share
No 1	1,200	
No 2	800	
No 3	600	
No 4	600	
No 5	500	
No 6	500	
No 7	450	
No 8	350	

The four-firm concentration ratio

You are required to calculate:

(a)   the market shares for each company.

(b)   the four-firm concentration ratio for this industry.   **(3 marks)**

14 **If the market supply curve for a good is inelastic, an increase in demand will:**

    A   Raise total sales proportionately more than it will raise the market price

    B   Raise total sales proportionately less than it will raise the market price

    C   Raise the market price but leave total sales unaffected

    D   Raise total sales but leave the market price unchanged   **(2 marks)**

15 **Mergers between businesses engaged in the same stage of production of a similar good or service are known as:**

    A   Horizontal mergers

    B   Conglomerate mergers

    C   Vertical mergers

    D   Cross mergers   **(2 marks)**

16   **A good which is characterised by both rivalry and excludability is called:**

   A   a public good

   B   a private good

   C   a government good

   D   an external good   **(2 marks)**

17   **The burden of an indirect tax on a good will fall more heavily on the producer when:**

   A   demand for the good is price elastic

   B   demand for the good is price inelastic

   C   demand for the good has unit elasticity

   D   supply of the good is price elastic   **(2 marks)**

18   **In practice a monopoly may have its market power limited by all of the following EXCEPT which ONE?**

   A   Countervailing power from its customers

   B   The market may be contestable

   C   There may be close substitutes for the good

   D   The firm's long run average cost curve may be falling   **(2 marks)**

19   **Which ONE of the following is the best example of a merit good?**

   A   Street lighting

   B   A national defence force

   C   Company cars for top sales executives

   D   A system of public libraries   **(2 marks)**

20   **There are three types of mergers**

   (i)   Horizontal mergers

   (ii) Vertical mergers

   (iii) Conglomerate mergers

   Match the following reasons for a merger with the appropriate type of merger listed above.

   A   To increase monopoly power and control over the market

   B   To ensure control over supplies of raw materials and components

   C   To secure economies of scale

   D   To reduce risk by diversifying the range of products sold and the range of markets

                                                                           (4 marks)

21 State whether the following statements about the privatisation of state industries are true or false.

Statement	True	False
(i) Privatisation increases the commercial pressure on the business to make a profit		
(ii) Privatisation ensures the business faces competition and so encourages greater efficiency		
(iii) Privatisation is a means of solving the principal—agent problem		
(iv) Privatisation is likely to make the business more responsive to needs of its customers		

(4 marks)

22 Which of the following are features of monopolistic competition?

(i) Large numbers of producers in the industry.

(ii) Differentiated products.

(iii) Companies producing at less than optimum output.

(iv) Monopoly profits in the long run.

A (i), (iii) and (iv) only

B (ii), (iii) and (iv)

C (i), (ii) and (iii) only

D (i), (ii) and (iv) only **(2 marks)**

23 The cobweb theorem:

A shows that, without intervention some agricultural prices will fall continuously over time

B explains why some agricultural prices are characterised by instability from one year to another

C shows that when some agricultural prices are disturbed, prices steadily return to their equilibrium level

D the imposition of minimum prices in agricultural products always lead to unsold surpluses **(2 marks)**

24 The necessary conditions for a firm to be able to practice price discrimination are:

(i)   The firm must be a price setter.

(ii)   The markets must be kept separate.

(iii)   The price elasticity of demand must be different in each market.

(iv)   Customers in each market must not be aware of the prices changed in other markets.

A   (i), (ii) and (iii) only

B   (i), (ii) and (iv) only

C   (ii), (iii) and (iv) only

D   all of them   **(2 marks)**

25 If an indirect tax is imposed on a good or service:

A   The price will rise by an amount equal to the tax

B   The producer decides on how much of the tax to pass on to the customer

C   The price rise will be smaller the greater is the price elasticity of demand

D   The price rise will be greater the smaller is the price elasticity of supply   **(2 marks)**

26 All of the following are examples of where externalities are likely to occur EXCEPT which ONE?

A   A business providing training schemes for its employees

B   Government expenditure on vaccination programmes for infectious diseases

C   Attending a concert given by a government funded orchestra

D   Private motorists driving cars in city centres   **(2 marks)**

27 Whenever government intervention prevents prices from reaching their equilibrium level, the result will always include ALL of the following EXCEPT which ONE?

A   Shortages or surpluses

B   Demand and supply not equal

C   Reduced profits for producers

D   Resources not allocated by price   **(2 marks)**

28 A rise in the price of a good accompanied by a fall in the quantity sold would result from

A   a decrease in supply

B   an increase in demand

C   a decrease in demand

D   an increase in supply   **(2 marks)**

29   The introduction of a national minimum wage will lead a business to reduce its number of employees most when

A   the demand for its final product is price elastic

B   wage costs are a small proportion of total costs

C   there is a low degree of substitutability between capital and labour

D   the supply of substitute factors of production is price inelastic   **(2 marks)**

30   The following is a list of different types of market structure.

- Perfect competition
- Monopolistic competition
- Oligopoly
- Monopoly

Match to each of the following situations the market structure that is being described.

Situation	Market structure
(i) In the long run, abnormal profits are competed away by the entry of new firms and for each firm output will be the optimum level of output	
(ii) The behaviour of any one firm is conditioned by how it expects its competitors to react to its price and output decisions	

(2 marks)

31   Which one of the following is NOT a characteristic of not-for-profit organisations?

A   They need efficient and effective management

B   They make financial surpluses and deficits

C   They have a range of stakeholders

D   The absence of any principal—agent problem   **(2 marks)**

32   In order to finance an excess of expenditure over taxation receipts, a government could:

A   reduce its current expenditure

B   issue government bonds

C   raise income tax

D   run an overdraft on its account with the World Bank   **(2 marks)**

33   A business could use all of the following to finance a lack of synchronisation in its short-term payments and receipts EXCEPT which ONE?

A   a bank overdraft

B   trade credit

C   its cash reserves

D   a hire purchase agreement   **(2 marks)**

34 State whether each of the following financial instruments appearing on a commercial bank's balance sheet is an asset or liability for the bank.

Instrument	Asset	Liability
Advances		
Money at call with discount houses		
Deposit accounts		
Shareholder capital		

(4 marks)

35 If banks are required to keep a reserve assets ratio of 10% and also wish to keep a margin of liquid reserves of 10%, by how much would deposits ultimately rise by if they acquire an additional $1000 of reserve assets?

A $10,000

B $5,000

C $1,000

D $500   **(2 marks)**

36 If a commercial bank reallocates some of its assets from less profitable to more profitable ones,

A   the bank's liquidity will be increased

B   the safety of the bank's assets will be increased

C   the bank's liquidity will be decreased

D   the liquidity and safety of the bank's assets will be unaffected   **(2 marks)**

37 Which of the following statements about the relationship between bond prices and bond yields is true?

A   They vary positively

B   They vary inversely

C   They vary inversely or positively depending on business conditions

D   They are not related   **(2 marks)**

38 Under a regime of flexible exchange rates, which one of the following would lead to a rise in the exchange rate for a country's currency?

A   a shift in the country's balance of payments current account   towards a surplus

B   a rise in interest rates in other countries

C   an increasing balance of trade deficit

D   the central bank buying foreign exchange on the foreign exchange market

(2 marks)

39   Exchange rates are determined by supply and demand for currencies in the foreign exchange market. State whether each of the following would be part of the supply of a country's currency or part of the demand for that country's currency.

Statement	Supply	Demand
Payments for imports into the country.		
Inflows of capital into the country.		
Purchases of foreign currency by the country's central bank.		

(2 marks)

40   Each of the following is a source of funds for capital investment for business except one. Which ONE is the EXCEPTION?

A   Commercial banks

B   Internally generated funds

C   The stock market

D   The central bank   **(2 marks)**

41   The linking of net savers with net borrowers is known as:

A   the savings function

B   financial intermediation

C   financial regulation

D   a store of value   **(2 marks)**

42   If a consumer price index rises, it shows that

A   the value of the currency has increased

B   real consumer income has fallen

C   all prices in the economy have risen

D   the purchasing power of money has decreased   **(2 marks)**

43   The main function of the money market is to

A   enable businesses and governments to obtain liquidity

B   encourage saving

C   permit the efficient buying and selling of shares

D   deal in credit instruments of more than one year maturity   **(2 marks)**

44   The effects of low real interest rates include all of the following EXCEPT which ONE?

A   Credit based sales will tend to be high

B   Nominal costs of borrowing will always below

C   Business activity will tend to increase

D   Investment will be encouraged   **(2 marks)**

45 **Which ONE of the following would cause the value of the multiplier to fall?**

A   A fall in the level of government expenditure

B   A rise in the marginal propensity to consume

C   A fall in business investment

D   A rise in the marginal propensity to save   **(2 marks)**

46 **The recession phase of the trade cycle will normally be accompanied by all of the following EXCEPT which ONE?**

A   A rise in the rate of inflation

B   A fall in the level of national output

C   An improvement in the trade balance

D   A rise in the level of unemployment   **(2 marks)**

47 **According to the classical school, in order to manage the economy governments should:**

A   use active fiscal and monetary policy

B   adopt a laissez faire approach and leave everything to market forces

C   announce monetary rules to control inflation, and liberalise product and factor markets

D   use only monetary policy to increase output and employment   **(2 marks)**

48 **The following is a list of types of unemployment.**

Structural unemployment

Cyclical unemployment

Real wage (classical) unemployment

Frictional unemployment.

Seasonal unemployment

Match the above types of unemployment to the following definitions.

Definition of unemployment	Type of unemployment
(i) Unemployment that occurs in particular industries and arises from long-term changes in the patterns of demand and supply	
(ii) Unemployment associated with industries or regions where the demand for labour and wage rates regularly rise and fall over the year	

(2 marks)

49 All of the following will lead to a fall in the level of economic activity in an economy EXCEPT which ONE?

A   A rise in cyclical unemployment

B   A fall in business investment

C   A decrease in government expenditure

D   A rise in interest rates   **(2 marks)**

50 The best measure of the standard of living in a country is

A   gross domestic product per capita

B   per capita personal consumption

C   gross national product per capita

D   personal disposable income   **(2 marks)**

51 Supply side policy is designed to

A   raise the level of aggregate monetary demand in the economy

B   manage the money supply in the economy

C   improve the ability of the economy to produce goods and services

D   reduce unemployment by limiting the supply of labour   **(2 marks)**

52 Indicate whether each of the following taxes are direct taxes or indirect taxes.

Type of tax	Direct	Indirect
Income tax		
Value added tax		
Corporation tax		
National insurance (social security tax)		

(4 marks)

53 International trade is best explained by the fact that:

A   all countries have an absolute advantage in the production of something

B   all countries have specialised in the production of certain goods and services

C   no country has an absolute advantage in the production of all goods and services

D   all countries have a comparative advantage in the production of something

(2 marks)

54   The following diagram shows the aggregate demand curve (AD) and the aggregate supply
      curve (AS) for an economy:

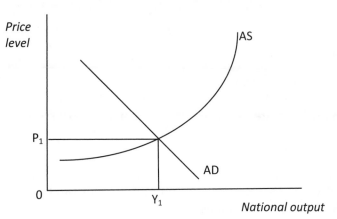

With reference to the diagram:

A .... supply shock would shift the .... curve to the left and cause the rate
of inflation to increase. However the level of .... would fall. A(n) .... fiscal
policy would shift the .... curve to the right leading to a .... in both the
level of national output and the rate of inflation.

Use the following words and phrases to fill in the gaps in the above passage.

positive

aggregate demand

rise

expansionary

negative

deflationary

aggregate supply

inflation

national output

fall   (6 marks)

55   **All of the following will encourage the process of the globalisation of production EXCEPT**
      which ONE?

      A   Reductions in international transport costs

      B   Higher levels of tariffs

      C   Reduced barriers to international capital movements

      D   Increased similarity in demand patterns between countries   **(2 marks)**

56 **Which ONE of the following shows the lowest degree of international mobility?**

    A   Unskilled labour

    B   Financial capital

    C   Technical knowledge

    D   Management   **(2 marks)**

57 **Identify which of the following statements about the balance of payments is true and which is false.**

Statement		True	False
(i)	A deficit on a country's balance of payments current account can be financed by a surplus of invisible earnings		
(ii)	Flows of profits and interest on capital appear in the Capital Account		
(iii)	Flexible exchange rate systems should, in principle, prevent persistent current account imbalances		
(iv)	Current account deficits tend to worsen in periods of rapid economic growth		

(4 marks)

58 **A fall in the exchange rate for a country's currency will improve the balance of payments current account if:**

    A   the price elasticity of demand for imports is greater than for exports

    B   the price elasticity of demand for exports is greater than for imports

    C   the sum of the price elasticities for imports and exports is less than one

    D   the sum of the price elasticities for imports and exports is greater than one

(2 marks)

59 **All of the following are benefits which all countries gain when adopting a single currency such as the Euro, EXCEPT which ONE?**

    A   Reduced transactions costs

    B   Increased price transparency

    C   Lower interest rates

    D   Reduced exchange rate uncertainty   **(2 marks)**

60   For each of the following events, indicate whether the direct effect of each on an economy would raise inflation, reduce inflation or leave the rate of inflation unaffected. Assume that the economy is close to full employment.

Event		Raise inflation	Lower inflation	Leave inflation unchanged
(i)	A rise (appreciation) in the exchange for the country's currency			
(ii)	A significant increase in the money supply			
(iii)	The removal of house prices from the consumer price index			
(iv)	A rise in business expectations leading to an increase in investment			

(4 marks)

61   **Compared to a fixed exchange rate system, an economy will benefit from a flexible exchange rate system because:**

A   it enables businesses to vary their export prices

B   governments will not have to deflate the economy when balance of payments deficits occur

C   it reduces the cost of acquiring foreign exchange

D   it ensures that businesses never become uncompetitive in international markets

(2 marks)

62   **All of the following statements are true EXCEPT which ONE?**

A   Import quotas tend to reduce prices

B   Trade protection tends to reduce consumer choice

C   Trade protection tends to reduce exports

D   Tariffs tend to reduce competition   **(2 marks)**

63   **Who are the gainers from inflation?**

(i)   Borrowers

(ii)   Savers

(iii)   Those who hold cash

(iv)   Those who invest in assets

A   (i), (ii)

B   (i), (iii)

C   (ii), (iii)

D   (i), (iv)   **(2 marks)**

Questions 64 and 65 are based on the following scenario:

Company X plc

Share price beginning of the year	£1.20
Share price end of the year	£1.50
Dividend paid	12 pence per share
Net profit before and after taxation	£25,000 and £20,000
No. of ordinary shares	100,000
Interest paid	£10,000

64 **The dividend yield was:**

A   7.5%

B   10%

C   12%

D   14%   **(2 marks)**

65 **The earnings per share was:**

A   5p

B   10p

C   15p

D   20p   **(2 marks)**

66 **Which one of the following will shift the supply curve for Good X to the right?**

A   A government subsidy in the production of Good X

B   A decrease in labour productivity in the production of Good X

C   An increase in the price of materials used to produce Good X

D   An increase in real wages paid to producers of Good X   **(2 marks)**

67 **Which of the following would be regarded as long-term capital?**

(i)   Ordinary shares

(ii)   Debentures

(iii) Convertible bond

A   (i) only

B   (i), (ii)

C   (ii), (iii)

D   (i), (ii), (iii)   **(2 marks)**

68   **Which of the following are examples of protectionism?**

(i)   Import quota

(ii)   Import tariff

(iii)   Export subsidy

A   (i) only

B   (i), (ii)

C   (ii), (iii)

D   (i), (ii) and (iii)   **(2 marks)**

69   **Which of the following would cause a withdrawal from the circular flow of funds?**

(i)   Increase in imports

(ii)   Increase in taxes

(iii)   Reduction in government expenditure

A   (i)

B   (i), (ii)

C   (i), (iii)

D   (i), (ii) and (iii)   **(2 marks)**

70   **If the central bank was to increase interest rates, what would be the least likely economic consequence?**

A   The exchange rate would rise

B   The price of non-financial assets would fall

C   Inflation should fall

D   Consumer expenditure would rise   **(2 marks)**

71   **Which ONE of the following is NOT a benefit from countries forming a monetary union and adopting a single currency?**

A   International transactions costs are reduced

B   Exchange rate uncertainty is removed

C   It economises on foreign exchange reserves

D   It allows each country to adopt an independent monetary policy   **(2 marks)**

72   **In the circular flow model of the economy, the level of national income will always reach an equilibrium because:**

A   injections and withdrawals are always equal

B   withdrawals are a function of the level of income

C   governments will change taxes and expenditure to ensure equilibrium

D   expenditure equals income   **(2 marks)**

73   **Which ONE of the following is an example of an external economy of scale for a business enterprise?**

    A   A locally available trained labour force

    B   Technical economies of scale

    C   Bulk buying

    D   Financial economies of scale   **(2 marks)**

74   **Diseconomies of scale occur in a business when:**

    A   minimum efficient scale is reached

    B   short-run variable costs begin to rise

    C   x-inefficiency exists

    D   long-run average costs begin to rise   **(2 marks)**

75   **What was the approximate level of sub-prime mortgages issued in the US in the run up to the banking crisis of 2008?**

    A $1.4 million

    B $14 million

    C $140 million

    D $1,400 million   **(2 marks)**

Section 6

MOCK ASSESSMENT 2

1   There has been a fall in the prices of raw materials that are used as inputs by all producers of a manufactured product that is sold in a perfectly competitive market for the finished product. Demand conditions for the final product are unchanged, and the demand curve has the normal negative slope. The effect of this change on the market price and quantity bought and sold of the final product will be:

    A   A higher price and higher quantity

    B   A lower price and lower quantity

    C   A lower price and higher quantity

    D   A higher price and lower quantity   **(2 marks)**

2   You observe that the price of a product has risen by 10% and its sales have fallen by 10%. Which one of the following on its own could have caused this?

    A   The demand curve has an elasticity greater (in absolute size) than –1

    B   A technical advance has shifted the supply curve to the right and demand elasticity is lose to –1

    C   The price of a substitute has fallen and supply elasticity is close to 1

    D   Wages paid by suppliers have risen so the supply curve has shifted to the left and demand elasticity is close to –1   **(2 marks)**

3   The price of a product falls from £100 to £99 and the quantity demanded rises from 1,000 to 1,100. Which one of the following is a true statement about the value of demand elasticity (as measured at the initial price and quantity)?

    A   Elasticity is –10

    B   Elasticity is –0.1

    C   Elasticity is –1

    D   Elasticity is +100   **(2 marks)**

4   Theatre attendances fell last year even though prices of admission also fell. Which one of the following on its own could explain this?

A   There was an increase in the supply of theatre seats but no change affecting demand conditions

B   There was an increased demand from consumers for visits to the theatre as the quality of TV deteriorated

C   There was a reduction in prices of cinema seats as many new multiplex cinemas opened up

D   There was an increase in the cost of putting on plays   **(2 marks)**

5   Which of the following is NOT a source of market failure:

A   Externalities

B   Common property resources

C   Asymmetric information

D   Constant returns to scale   **(2 marks)**

6   There has been a fall in input prices for all producers of a good sold in a competitive industry. Assuming this is a normal good, the effect of this change on market price and quantity will be (choose only one).

A   A higher price and higher quantity

B   A lower price and lower quantity

C   A lower price and higher quantity

D   A higher price and lower quantity   **(2 marks)**

7   The price of a product rises from £20 to £22 and the quantity demanded falls from 10,000 to 9,000. Which one of the following is a true statement about the value of demand elasticity (as measured at the initial price and quantity)?

A   Elasticity is –0.1

B   Elasticity is –1

C   Elasticity is –0.5

D   Elasticity is –2   **(2 marks)**

8 A firm can sell its product for £40 each in a competitive output market, its total cost of production for the production range of 400 units to 405 units is given below:

400	401	402	403	404
£12,600	£12,630	£12,665	£12,730	£12,900

What is the profit maximising level of production?

A   401

B   402

C   403

D   404   **(2 marks)**

9 The price of coffee beans rose by 5% last year and quantity purchased rose by 5%.

A   There was an increase in supply as a result of new production techniques but not changes in conditions of demand

B   Consumer incomes increased substantially and coffee is a normal good

C   The price of cocoa fell substantially and cocoa is a substitute for coffee

D   There was a major frost in Brazil that reduced its coffee production, and Brazil has a big share of world production   **(2 marks)**

10 Brand X sold 500,000 items at £200 each last year. It is known that its price elasticity of demand is -0.5 (calculated at the current price and quantity). What would sales be this year if there are no other changes affecting demand and the price per unit is raised to £220?

A   475,000

B   400,000

C   450,000

D   525,000   **(2 marks)**

11 A firm can sell its product for £25 each in a competitive output market. Its total cost of production for the production range of 200 units to 205 units is given below:

200	201	202	203	204	205
£3,600	£3,615	£3,634	£3,658	£3,688	£3,720

What is the profit maximising level of production?

A   201

B   202

C   203

D   204   **(2 marks)**

12   Which of the following is NOT a source of market failure?

A   Public goods

B   Common property resources

C   Inefficient exclusion

D   Diminishing returns to scale   **(2 marks)**

13   A scarce resource is one for which:

A   Opportunity cost is high

B   The demand at zero price would exceed supply

C   Demand always exceeds supply

D   There is a finite supply   **(2 marks)**

14   Prices are most volatile when:

A   Supply is elastic, demand is elastic

B   Supply is inelastic, demand is inelastic

C   Supply is elastic, demand is inelastic

D   Supply is inelastic, demand is elastic   **(2 marks)**

15   What do economists mean by the term opportunity cost?

A   The value of the best alternative use for a resource

B   The price equilibrium of the scarce good

C   The cost of allocating scarce resources

D   None of the above   **(2 marks)**

16   Which one of the following will shift the supply curve for Good B to the right?

A   An increase in the subsidy paid to produce Good B

B   A reduction in labour productivity while producing Good B

C   An increase in the price of raw materials used to produce Good B

D   An increase in wages paid to workers who produce Good B   **(2 marks)**

17   A minimum price is set for Good X at £100 which is below the free market price. A
decrease in the supply of Good X, keeping the minimum price fixed at £100 will result in:

A   A rise in price and a surplus of Good X

B   A rise in price and a shortage of Good X

C   A rise in price and a balance between supply and demand for Good X

D   No change in price and a shortage of Good X   **(2 marks)**

18   **Which one of the following is not a feature of a free market?**

A   Demand

B   Supply

C   Prices

D   Government intervention   **(2 marks)**

19   **A car manufacturer acquiring a car dealership is an example of:**

A   Horizontal integration – forward

B   Horizontal integration – backwards

C   Vertical integration – forward

D   Vertical integration – backwards   **(2 marks)**

20   **Which of the following is a natural barrier to entry?**

A   High entry cost

B   Patent

C   Government regulation

D   Nationalisation   **(2 marks)**

21   **Which of the following is associated with monopolistic competition?**

A   Barriers to entry

B   Economies of scale

C   Excess capacity

D   None of the above   **(2 marks)**

22   **To belong to a cartel in the model of oligopoly, firms have got to 'abide by the rules'. These rules are:**

A   To stick to the price and the output that is set by the cartel

B   To stick to the price but not the output that is set by the cartel

C   To stick to the output but not the price that is set by the cartel

D   There are no formal rules when joining a cartel   **(2 marks)**

23   **The expenditure method of measuring national income:**

A   Measures economic activity by summing the value of expenditure on consumer goods

B   Measures economic activity by summing of expenditure on final goods

C   Measures economic activity by summing the value of expenditure on all goods

D   Is determined by the income method   **(2 marks)**

24 **Net national product is equal to:**

A GDP less net property income from abroad less depreciation

B GDP plus net property income from abroad

C GDP less depreciation

D GDP plus net property income from abroad less depreciation **(2 marks)**

25 **A world recession is likely to lead to:**

A A leftward shift in a country's macroeconomic demand schedule

B A rightward shift in a country's short-run aggregate supply curve

C A rightward shift in a country's macroeconomic demand schedule

D A leftward shift in a country's short-run aggregate supply curve **(2 marks)**

26 **Consider the following data for country Y:**

Year 20X8	NI	£500m	PI 100
Year 20X9	NI	£600m	PI 120

where NI = national income and where PI = price index. In real terms, the economy between 20X8 and 20X9:

A Rose by £100 million

B Rose by £120 million

C Fell by £20 million

D Remained the same **(2 marks)**

27 **An economy is made up of three firms. Firm A mines a raw material, it pays £200 to its workers and it sells £200 worth of output to firm B and £300 worth to firm C (it has no other sales or costs). Firm B makes a consumer good and sells £400 worth, paying £200 to its workers. Firm C also makes a consumer good, selling £600 worth and paying its workers £200. There are no transactions between firms B and C. What is the value of GDP?**

A £1,200

B £800

C £1,000

D £700 **(2 marks)**

28 **The short-run aggregate supply curve is positively sloped because:**

A Input prices rise as output expands

B With given input prices, firms' unit costs rise with output

C Firms are faced with increasing returns to scale

D Input prices rise when there is an inflationary gap **(2 marks)**

29   If the economy starts at potential GDP, has a positively sloped short run aggregate supply curve, and there is an exogenous increase in export demand, the effects will be:

   A   In the short run, output will rise while prices fall and in the long run prices will return to the original position and GDP will be higher

   B   In the short run, there will be some increase in GDP and some in prices, but in the long-run there will be higher prices but no increase in GDP

   C   In the short run, there will be some fall in GDP and prices, but both will return to their starting point in the long run

   D   In the short run, prices will rise while GDP falls, and both will return to their initial position in the long run   **(2 marks)**

30   Which of the following statements about the balance of payments is NOT correct?

   A   Payments that lead to demands for foreign currency are measured as debits, while payments that lead to supplies of foreign exchange are measured as credits

   B   The current account balance plus the capital and financial account balances add up to zero

   C   A current account deficit is a sign of a weak economy, while a current account surplus is a sign of a strong economy

   D   A current account surplus implies that domestic residents are increasing their net foreign assets   **(2 marks)**

31   The government is concerned about the high level of voluntary unemployment within the economy. Which of the following policies would be most appropriate to deal with this problem?

   A   Reduce minimum wages

   B   Increase unemployment benefit

   C   Reduce the level of taxes on income

   D   Reduce the level of taxes on expenditure   **(2 marks)**

32   The aggregate demand curve is negatively sloped because:

   A   Firms will only produce more at higher prices

   B   Input prices rise as output increases

   C   Tax revenue rises at higher prices

   D   Consumer spending falls at higher price levels owing to the fall in real value of their savings, and net exports fall as domestic goods' prices rise relative to foreign prices
                                                                                (2 marks)

33   An economy is made up of three firms. Firm A mines a raw material, it pays £200 to its workers and it sells £600 worth of output to firm B and £800 worth to firm C (it has no other sales or costs). Firm B makes a consumer good and sells £1,400 worth, paying £400 to its workers. Firm C also makes a consumer good, selling £2,200 worth and paying its workers £800. There are no transactions between firms B and C, and there are no taxes or government spending, and no imports and exports. What is the value of GDP?

A   £2,400

B   £3,600

C   £2,000

D   £2,300   (2 marks)

34   Which of the following must always balance?

A   Visible balance

B   Invisible balance

C   Capital account

D   The balance of payments   (2 marks)

35   Which of the following explains why countries may benefit from international trade, according to the principle of comparative advantage?

A   By specialising in production of goods, which can be made relatively cheaply, and trading with others who specialise in producing different products, all can become better off

B   Trade involves domestic jobs moving to countries that have cheaper labour, and this means that the country with high priced labour is worse off as a result

C   Specialisation and trade only works under the protection of tariffs

D   Nations can only benefit from international trade if some other country loses
                                                                       (2 marks)

36   Which of the following items would be counted as part of national income?

(i)   Child allowance

(ii)   A housekeeper's salary

(iii) The pay of a fire officer.

A   (i) and (ii)

B   (ii) and (iii)

C   (i) only

D   (ii) only   (2 marks)

37   The accelerator principle states that:

Investment is increased when interest rates fall.

A   An increase in consumer demand leads to a more than proportionate increase in the level of investment

B   An increase in investment will lead to a more than proportionate increase in output

C   The rate of change of investment affects the rate of change of output   **(2 marks)**

38   **Household saving is equal to:**

A   Disposable income less taxes and consumption expenditure

B   Disposable income less imports, taxes and consumption expenditure

C   Disposable income less imports and consumption expenditure

D   Disposable income less consumption expenditure   **(2 marks)**

39   **If in a closed economy, consumption expenditure increases from £18,000 to £19,500 when national income increases from £20,000 to £26,000, then the marginal propensity to consume out of national income is:**

A   0.25 and the multiplier is 1.33

B   0.75 and the multiplier is 1.33

C   0.25 and the multiplier is 2

D   0.75 and the multiplier is 2   **(2 marks)**

40   **A fall in real gross domestic product would result from an increase in all of the following except:**

A   Savings

B   Imports

C   Taxation

D   Government expenditure   **(2 marks)**

41   **The difference in the shape of the short-run and the long-run aggregate supply curve can be explained by the assumption that:**

A   Capital is fixed in the short run but variable in the long run

B   Money illusion exists in the short run but not in the long run

C   The Central Bank can control the supply of money in the long run

D   Wage constraints are fixed in the long run   **(2 marks)**

42   According to Keynes:

A   Both transactions and speculative demand for money are a function of income

B   Both transactions and speculative demand for money are a function of interest rates

C   Transactions demand is a function of income, speculative demand is a function of interest rates

D   Transactions demand is a function of interest rates, speculative demand is a function of income   **(2 marks)**

43   Which of the following is NOT an example of short-term finance?

A   Bank overdraft

B   Trade credit

C   Venture capital

D   Factoring   **(2 marks)**

44   Which of the following financial institutions would be associated with the money market?

(i)   Banks.

(ii)   Discount houses.

(iii)   Investment trusts.

(iv)   Unit trusts.

A   (i) and (ii)

B   (i) and (iii)

C   (ii) and (iii)

D   (ii) and (iv)   **(2 marks)**

45   If a discount house offered the Central Bank £95 for a £100 short-term (90 days) gilt, the approximate annual rate of return would be:

A   5%

B   10%

C   15%

D   21%   **(2 marks)**

46   If the government were frightened that the economy is going to enter a recession, the best course of action would be:

A   Raise interest rates, raise the reserve asset ratio

B   Lower interest rates, lower the reserve asset ratio

C   Raise interest rates, lower the reserve asset ratio

D   Lower interest rates, raise the reserve asset ratio   **(2 marks)**

47   A sudden discrete fall in the fixed exchange rate which the government commits itself to defend is called a:

   A   Revaluation

   B   Appreciation

   C   Devaluation

   D   Depreciation   **(2 marks)**

48   Assuming a floating exchange rate system in the USA, if the level of US short-term interest rates falls, the exchange rate of the dollar will:

   A   Rise and stay at its new higher level

   B   Rise in the short term and then fall back close to its previous level

   C   Fall and stay at its new lower level

   D   Fall in the short term and then rise back close to its previous level   **(2 marks)**

49   Which of the following best characterises the views of a monetarist?

   A   In the long term, unemployment can be reduced by an expansionary fiscal policy

   B   In the long term, unemployment can be reduced by an expansionary monetary policy

   C   In the long term, unemployment can be reduced by increasing efficiency and productivity

   D   In the long term, unemployment can be reduced but only at the cost of a higher rate of inflation   **(2 marks)**

50   If the UK's current account balance is in deficit by £7bn, its capital account in surplus by £4bn, and sales of foreign exchange reserves amount to £2bn:

   A   The UK can repay £1bn of IMF loans

   B   The UK needs additional IMF loans of £1bn

   C   The UK can repay £5bn of IMF loans

   D   The UK needs additional IMF loans of £5bn   **(2 marks)**

51   The advantages of fixed exchange rates include:

   (i)   Monetary policy is more effective.

   (ii)   There will be no need to hold gold reserves.

   (iii) Fiscal policy is more effective.

   A   (i) and (ii)

   B   (ii) and (iii)

   C   (i) only

   D   (iii) only   **(2 marks)**

52   **Which of the following organisations were rescued by government intervention in 2007 and 2008?**

(i)   Lehman Brothers

(ii)   AIG

(iii)   Northern Rock

A   (i) and (ii)

B   (ii) and (iii)

C   (i) only

D   (iii) only   **(2 marks)**

53   **One of the contributory factors of the 2008 banking crisis was the fact that mortgage lenders were able to effectively sell on their mortgage books via the issue of three tier bonds. What was the name given to these bonds?**

A   Collateralised debt obligations (CDOs)

B   Credit default swaps (CDSs)

C   Convertible bond warrants (CBWs)

D   Rainbow bonds   **(2 marks)**

54   **If inflation is low and a country is facing a recession, then the government (or central bank) will often look to reduce interest rates to boost the economy. However, in the UK between 2007 and 2010 interest rates were already very low so the UK government chose to boost the economy by printing £200 million and injecting the funds into the financial system. What is the technical term for this?**

A   Structural debt reduction

B   Debt realignment

C   Quantitative easing

D   Fiscal engineering   **(2 marks)**

55   **A company is considering purchasing a new machine for £25,000. This would increase the annual cash flow of the company by £6,500 in each of the next six years. If the cost of capital is 9 per cent per annum, the net present value of this investment is:**

A   £4,159

B   £10,780

C   £10,901

D   £14,000   **(2 marks)**

56 Which one of the following would not be a stakeholder for a mutual society?

A   shareholders

B   customers

C   employees

D   managers   **(2 marks)**

57 A good which is characterised by both rivalry and excludability is known as:

A   A merit good

B   A public good

C   A private good

D   None of the above   **(2 marks)**

58 If the reserve asset ratio was 40%, how much money could a bank create from an initial deposit of £1,000?

A   £2,000

B   £2,500

C   £4,000

D   £10,000   **(2 marks)**

59 If money supply is £200 million, velocity of circulation is 5, transactions demand £250 million, what is the average price level?

A   3

B   4

C   5

D   6   **(2 marks)**

60 During the 20th century in the U.K., workers lost their jobs in the coal and steel industries as supply shifted to countries with lower costs. This is an example of which type of unemployment?

A   Cyclical

B   Structural

C   Seasonal

D   Frictional   **(2 marks)**

61 Which of the following is not an example of supply side economics?

A Privatisation

B Lower state benefits

C Lower direct taxes

D Increased government expenditure **(2 marks)**

62 Which of the following are examples of government non-marketable debt?

(i) Treasury Bills

(ii) Gilt-edged Stocks

(iii) National Savings Certificates

(iv) Premium Bonds

A (i), (ii)

B (i), (iii)

C (ii), (iv)

D (iii), (iv) **(2 marks)**

63 An American imported car cost £100,000 last year in the U.K. when the sterling /dollar exchange rate was £1 = $2. The exchange rate is now £1 = $1.50 and the dollar price has risen by 10%. What is the sterling price of this car today?

A £150,000

B £146,666

C £120,000

D £100,000 **(2 marks)**

64 Which of the following statements is correct?

A Not-for-profit organisations are only found in the public sector

B Not-for-profit organisations are only found in the private sector

C Not-for-profit organisations can be found in both the public and the private sector

D Not-for-profit organisations cannot survive without profits **(2 marks)**

65 If the central bank raised interest rates, what would the most likely outcome on share prices be?

A A fall in share prices

B A rise in share prices

C No change in share prices

D Impossible to tell **(2 marks)**

66   The original Phillips curve suggests that there is

A   an inverse relationship between the rate of inflation and the level of unemployment

B   a direct relationship between the rate of inflation and the level of unemployment

C   an inverse relationship between the rate of inflation and the money supply

D   a direct relationship between the rate of inflation and the money supply   **(2 marks)**

67   **Governments wish to control inflation because**

A   it redistributes from rich to poor people

B   it damages international competitiveness

C   it reduces government tax revenue

D   it reduces unemployment   **(2 marks)**

68   **The main advantage of a system of flexible or floating exchange rates is that it:**

A   provides certainty for those engaged in international trade

B   provides discipline for government economic management

C   reduces international transaction costs

D   provides automatic correction of balance of payments

69   **Discounting a future stream of income means:**

A   taking into account possible future falls in the stream of income

B   ignoring yearly fluctuations in income and taking the average

C   reducing the value of future income streams because future income is worth less than current income

D   increasing the value of future income streams to take account of the effect of inflation   **(2 marks)**

70   **Which of the following is not a prime objective of corporate governance?**

A   to control directors' activities

B   to improve the way companies are run

C   to improve employee's working conditions

D   to protect shareholder interests   **(2 marks)**

71   **The main objective of the WTO is:**

A   to raise living standards in developing countries

B   to minimise barriers to international trade

C   to harmonise tariffs

D   to eliminate customs unions   **(2 marks)**

72 **A $100 stock with market price of $90 and a dividend of $6 will generate a yield of:**

A 6%

B 6.67%

C 7.5%

D 15.0% **(2 marks)**

73 **A French manufacturer who imports components from the US is struggling to compete against other French competitors due to a weak Euro making imported components more expensive. What type of exchange risk is being described here?**

A economic risk

B transaction risk

C translation risk **(2 marks)**

74 **Cyclical unemployment refers to unemployment**

A which occurs because of the seasonal nature of some industries

B resulting from the long-term decline of an industry

C which occurs at particular times of the year

D which occurs during recessions **(2 marks)**

75 **The linking of net savers with net borrowers is known as:**

A the savings function

B financial intermediation

C financial regulation

D a store of value **(2 marks)**

Section 7

ANSWERS TO MOCK ASSESSMENT 1

1 ROCE = 105/1,000 × 100% = **10.5%**

2 C

3

(a) NPV = −$7,000 + ($2,000/1.10) + ($3,000/1.10^2) + ($2,500/1.10^3) = −$824

(b) No

(c) NPV = −$7,000 + ($2,000/1.06) + ($3,000/1.06^2) + ($3,000/1.06^3) = $76

4 C

5

The *stakeholders* in a company are all those who have an interest in the strategy and behaviour of the *company*. Their interest may not always coincide with those of the *shareholders* who are principally interested in *profits*. The task of management is to attempt to reconcile these conflicting interests.

6 B

7

Economic process	Raise curve	Lower curve	Leave curve unaffected
A rise in wage costs	X		
Increase opportunities for economies of scale			X
A fall in the price of raw materials		X	
A shift in the demand curve to the left			X

8

Statement	True	False
The law of diminishing returns shows how long run cost tends to rise if the scale of output becomes too great		X
A firm's short run cost curve is always U shaped; the long cost curve may or may not be	X	
For most firms technological change is one of the most important economies of scale		X
Economies of scale act as barrier to entry to industries	X	

9

Characteristic	Yes	No
A large number of small firms		X
A preference for non-price competition over price competition	X	
Interdependence of decision making	X	
Ease of entry and exit to and from the industry		X

10

Statement	True	False
Collusion is more likely in oligopoly markets than in other markets	X	
If there are economies of scale, a monopoly firm may charge lower prices than equivalent firms facing competition	X	
Oligopolistic firms can never achieve lower long run costs than could competitive firms in the same industry		X
Oligopolistic firms can make excess profits but only in the short run		X

11 **B**

12 **A**

13

Company	Sales	Market share (in %)
No 1	1,200	24
No 2	800	16
No 3	600	12
No 4	600	12
No 5	500	10
No 6	500	10
No 7	450	9
No 8	350	7
The four-firm concentration ratio	64%	

14   **B**

15   **A**

16   **B**

17   **A**

18   **D**

19   **D**

20

(a)   (i)   Horizontal merger

(b)   (ii)   Vertical merger

(c)   (i)   Horizontal merger

(d)   (iii)   Conglomerate merger

21

Statement		True	False
(i)	Privatisation increases the commercial pressure on the business to make a profit	X	
(ii)	Privatisation ensures the business faces competition and so encourages greater efficiency		X
(iii)	Privatisation is a means of solving the principal—agent problem		X
(iv)	Privatisation is likely to make the business more responsive to needs of its customers	X	

22 **C**

23 **B**

24 **A**

25 **C**

26 **C**

27 **C**

28 **A**

29 **A**

30

Situation		Market structure
(i)	In the long run, abnormal profits are competed away by the entry of new firms and for each firm output will be the optimum level of output	*Perfect competition*
(ii)	The behaviour of any one firm is conditioned by how it expects its competitors to react to its price and output decisions	*Oligopoly*

31 **D**

32 **B**

33 **D**

34

Instrument	Asset	Liability
Advances	X	
Money at call with discount houses	X	
Deposit accounts		X
Shareholder capital		X

35 **B**

36 **C**

37   B

38   A

39

Statement	Supply	Demand
Payments for imports into the country	X	
Inflows of capital into the country		X
Purchases of foreign currency by the country's central bank	X	

40   D

41   B

42   D

43   A

44   B

45   D

46   A

47   C

48

Definition of unemployment		Type of unemployment
(i)	Unemployment that occurs in particular industries and arises from long-term changes in the patterns of demand and supply	*Structural unemployment*
(ii)	Unemployment associated with industries or regions where the demand for labour and wage rates regularly rise and fall over the year	*Seasonal unemployment*

49   A

50   B

51   C

52

Type of tax	Direct	Indirect
Income tax	X	
Value added tax		X
Corporation tax	X	
National insurance (social security tax)	X	

53   **D**

54   A *negative* supply shock would shift the *aggregate supply* curve to the left and cause the rate of inflation to increase. However the level of *national output* would fall. An *expansionary* fiscal policy would shift the *aggregate demand* curve to the right leading to a rise in both the level of national output and the rate of inflation.

55   **B**

56   **A**

57

Statement		True	False
(i)	A deficit on a country's balance of payments current account can be financed by a surplus of invisible earnings		X
(ii)	Flows of profits and interest on capital appear in the Capital Account		X
(iii)	Flexible exchange rate systems should, in principle, prevent persistent current account imbalances	X	
(iv)	Current account deficits tend to worsen in periods of rapid economic growth	X	

58   **D**

59   **C**

60

	Event	Raise inflation	Lower inflation	Leave inflation unchanged
(i)	A rise (appreciation) in the exchange for the country's currency		X	
(ii)	A significant increase in the money supply	X		
(iii)	The removal of house prices from the consumer price index			X
(iv)	A rise in business expectations leading to an increase in investment	X		

61 **B**

62 **A**

63 **D**

Borrowers and those who hold assets gain from inflation.

64 **B**

Dividend yield

= Share price beginning of year £1.20

Dividend paid 12p

= 10%

65 **D**

Earnings per share = $\dfrac{£20,000}{100,000}$

= 20p

66 **A**

A government subsidy would shift the supply curve to the right since it makes the product cheaper.

67 **D**

Ordinary shares, debentures and convertible bonds are all examples of long-term capital.

68 **D**

Import quotas, import tariffs and export subsidies are all examples of protectionism.

69   D

An increase in imports, an increase in taxes and a reduction in government expenditure would all constitute a withdrawal from the circular flow of income.

70   B

If the central bank was to increase interest rates, consumer expenditure would fall.

71   D

Countries in a monetary union and adopting a single currency cannot have independent monetary policies. In the eurozone, monetary policy is controlled by the ECB (European Central Bank).

72   B

A, C and D are not true. Equilibrium will be reached when withdrawals adjust to match any changes in injections

73   A

B, C and D are examples of internal economies of scale (economics of scale that accrue to the firm because the firm itself gets bigger).

74   D

Diseconomies of scale are factors which cause the LRAC to increase as output increases.

75   D

Section 8

ANSWERS TO MOCK ASSESSMENT 2

1   C

If there has been a fall in the price of raw materials, this should result in a fall in price, which will lead to more being purchased.

2   D

If price has risen by 10%, this indicates a shift to the left in the supply curve and if demand has also fallen by 10%, this indicates that price elasticity of demand is near −1.

3   A

Change in demand +100

Change in price −1

% Change +10

% Change −1

So −10.

4   C

Reduction in price can be explained by increase in supply, so A or C. Alternative A states that demand stays the same, so by process of elimination answer must be C.

5   D

Constant returns to scale are often a feature of a market or industry but they are not a source of market failure in the way of, say monopoly power.

6   C

This is very similar to question 1, using the same rationale. Answer C.

7   B

Demand   % Fall   −10%

Price   % Rise   +10%

Answer − 1, so B.

8   B

We can work out total revenue at each output and subtract total cost at each output, but this is time consuming.

9   B

The only possible answer here that has both price and demand increasing would be for the demand curve to move to the right – i.e. consumer incomes increased substantially.

10   A

If price is raised from £200 to £220, this is a 10% price increase.

If elasticity of demand is –0.5, then there has been a 5% reduction in demand. 5% of 500,000 is equal to 25,000.

So answer is A – 475,000.

11   C

12   D

Similar to question 10. Diminishing returns is a feature of many industries but is not an example of market failure.

13   B

Non-economists might have gone for alternative D, but B is technically the correct answer.

14   B

On a question like this, draw a diagram on a scrap piece of paper. Where demand and supply are inelastic, adjustment comes on price. Where they are elastic, adjustment comes on quantity. So volatility will occur when they are both inelastic.

15   A

Only one answer here, the value of the best alternative use for a resource.

16   A

A shift to the right in a supply curve indicates an increase in supply which could only be caused by an increase in the subsidy paid to produce the good.

17   C

Setting the minimum price below the original free market equilibrium price has no effect on the original equilibrium, so price is determined by supply and demand.

A decrease in supply will shift supply to the left. This will increase equilibrium price and reduce equilibrium quantity, therefore there will be a balance between supply and demand.

18   D

Government intervention is not a feature of a free market since this market is determined by consumers and producers.

19   C

20   A

A natural barrier to entry is one which happens through economic forces, e.g. economies of scale. Alternatives B, C and D are all barriers created by governments.

21   C

One of the most prevalent features of all imperfect markets is excess capacity. This happens because the profit maximising output is reached when the average cost curve is still falling.

22   A

In a cartel, it is the cartel which sets both price and output.

23   B

The expenditure method of measuring national income measures economic activity by summing the value of expenditure on final goods.

24   D

Net national product is equal to gross domestic product + net property income from abroad less depreciation.

25   A

A world recession is likely to lead to a leftward shift in a country's macroeconomic demand schedule.

26   D

We need to convert £600m into 20X8 prices, so:

$$£600m \times \frac{100}{120} = £500m$$

So, in real terms, the economy between 20X8 and 20X9 remained the same.

27   C

In order to calculate a question like this, we can either add the value on at each stage or take the value of the final product. The latter is easier.

So:	Firm B is worth	£400
	Firm C is worth	£600
	Firm A is not included	———
		£1,000

28   B

The short-run aggregate supply curve is positively sloped because, with given input prices, firms' unit costs rise with output.

29   B

In the short run, there will be some increase in GDP and some in prices but in the long run, there will be higher prices but no increase in GDP.

30   C

The statement which is incorrect is that a current account deficit is a sign of weakness, while a surplus is a sign of strength.

31   C

This is a supply side issue, so reductions in income tax would increase the incentive to work.

32   D

The aggregate demand curve is negatively sloped because consumer spending falls at higher price levels owing to the fall in the real value of their savings, and net exports fall as domestic goods' prices rise relative to foreign prices.

33   B

From B £1,400 + Firm C £2,200 = £3,600.

34   D

The balance of payments itself must balance. A surplus will be reflected in an inflow of currency and reserves, a deficit will show an outflow.

35   A

The principle of comparative advantage is that by specialising in production of goods which can be made relatively cheaply and trading with others who specialise in producing different products, all can become better off.

36   B

In order to be counted as part of national income, there must be an expenditure, an output and an income which would include a housekeeper's salary and the pay of a fire officer but not child allowance.

So (ii) and (iii) – Answer B.

37   B

The accelerator principle states that an increase in consumer demand leads to a more than proportionate increase in the level of investment.

38 D

Household saving is equal to disposable income less consumption expenditure.

39 A

$$MPC = \frac{1,500}{6,000} = 0.25$$

$$\text{Multiplier } = \frac{1}{1-0.25} = \frac{1}{0.75}$$

$$= 1.33$$

40 D

Alternatives A, B and C are all withdrawals, government expenditure is an injection, so an increase in G would cause real GDP to rise.

41 D

The difference in the shape of the short-run and the long-run aggregate supply curve can be explained by the assumption that wage constraints are fixed in the long run.

42 C

According to Keynes, transactions demand for money is a function of income and speculative demand is a function of interest rates.

43 C

Venture capital is similar to share capital in that it is a long-term liability.

44 A

The money market is concerned with short-term finance, the capital market is concerned with the long term. So answer is banks and discount houses.

So A – (i) and (ii).

45

If you are receiving a £5 rate of return on a £95 investment, this equates to approximately 5.26% over 3 months. So the approximate annual rate is 5.26% × 4 = 21.04%.

This makes alternative D the closest.

46 B

If the government wants to avoid recession, it should lower interest rates to encourage investment and lower the reserve asset ratio to give banks more liquidity.

47 C

A sudden discrete fall in the fixed exchange rate which the government commits itself to defend is called a devaluation.

48 D

In the short term the exchange rate will fall but, in the long term, it should revert back to its purchasing parity.

49 C

Monetarists believe that in the long term, unemployment can be reduced by increasing efficiency and productivity.

50 B

If current account is in deficit by £7bn and capital account is in surplus of £4bn, overall deficit is £3bn. If we sell reserves of £2bn, there is still shortfall of £1bn which we could borrow from IMF.

51 D

Of the alternatives given, only fiscal policy is more effective since interest rates are pegged to international levels ensuring that crowding out does not happen.

52 B

53 A

54 C

55 A

NPV = (£6,500 × Annuity factor) – £25,000 = (£6,500 × 4.486) – £25,000 = £4,159

56 A

Response (A) is the correct answer as a mutual society does not have shareholders but is owned collectively by its customers, for example a mutual building society is owned by its depositors.

57 C

A good which is characterised by both rivalry and excludability is known as a private good.

58   **B**

$$\frac{1}{0.4} = 2.5$$

$2.5 \times £1,000 = £2,500.$

59   **B**

MV = PT, so P = MV/T = 200 × 5/250 = 4

60   **B**

This was caused by changes in the structure of industry.

61   **D**

Increasing government expenditure changes demand not supply.

62   **D**

National Savings Certificates and Premium Bonds are examples of government non-marketable debt.

63   **B**

At £1 = $2 dollar price was $200,000, if dollar price has risen by 10% it is now $220,000. At an exchange rate of £1 = $1.50 sterling price is now

$$\frac{$220,000}{1.5} = £146,666$$

64   **C**

Not-for-profit organisations can be found in both sectors, for example private sector charity and public sector local authority.

65   **A**

By considering the share price as being explained by the present value of future cash flows, an increase in interest rates will raise borrowing costs which will result in a higher discount rate to apply to cash flows. Hence the share price will fall.

66   **A**

The original Phillips curve suggests that there is an inverse relationship between the rate of inflation and the level of unemployment.

67   **B**

If governments were seeking to reduce unemployment, they should reduce interest rates and lower taxes.

68   D

The main advantage of a system of flexible or floating exchange rates is that it provides automatic correction of balance of payments.

69   C

Responses (A) and (B) are concerned with the absolute value of income streams and not discounting those streams. Response (C) is correct since discounting is done because future income is worth less now even in the absence of inflation. Response (D) does not relate to discounting.

70   C

While governance would ensure compliance with relevant legislation concerning employee working conditions, the primary focus is not employees per se.

71   B

The WTO is an organisation concerned with trade agreements and associated matters, and seeks a reduction in barriers to trade. The minimalisation of trade barriers is its primary aim. The WTO may see the others as desirable, but they are not its direct concerns.

72   B

Yield = 6/90 × 100% = 6.67%

73   A

By definition.

74   D

A and C are seasonal unemployment, B is structural.

75   B

Financial intermediaries link borrowers with savers.